The FIRST
ENGLISH DICTIONARY
1604

A

Table Alphabeticall, conteyning and teaching the true vvriting, and vnderstanding of hard vsuall English wordes, borrowed from the Hebrew, Greeke, Latine, or French. &c.

With the interpretation thereof by *plaine English words, gathered for the benefit & helpe of Ladies, Gentlewomen, or any other vnskilfull persons.*

Whereby they may the more easilie and better vnderstand many hard English wordes, vvhich they shall heare or read in Scriptures, Sermons, or elswhere, and also be made able to vse the same aptly themselues.

Legere, et non intelligere, neglegere est.
As good not read, as not to vnderstand.

AT LONDON,
Printed by I. R. for Edmund Weauer, & are to be sold at his shop at the great North doore of Paules Church.
1 6 04.

The FIRST
ENGLISH
DICTIONARY

1604

ROBERT CAWDREY'S
A TABLE ALPHABETICAL

INTRODUCTION BY
JOHN SIMPSON
CHIEF EDITOR
OXFORD ENGLISH DICTIONARY

The First English Dictionary, 1604
Robert Cawdrey's A Table Alphabeticall

First published in 2007 by the Bodleian Library
Broad Street, Oxford OX1 3BG

This edition made from the sole surviving copy of the first printing in 1604 of
A Table Alphabeticall by Robert Cawdrey, now in the Bodleian Library, shelfmark
Arch. A f. 141 (2).

www.bodleianbookshop.co.uk

ISBN 1 85124 385 2
ISBN 13 978 1 85124 385 3

Introduction © John Simpson 2007
Text © Bodleian Library, University of Oxford 2007
Jacket illustration © Clifford Harper 2007

Image © Bodleian Library, University of Oxford 2007

Designed by Melanie Gradtke and Dot Little
Printed and bound by Biddles Ltd, Norfolk
British Library Catalogue in Publishing
A CIP record of this publication is available from the British Library

INTRODUCTION

The story of Robert Cawdrey is a fascinating one, and one which is only slowly coming to light. Until recently our knowledge of him was based almost exclusively on sketchy details found in the dedication to his dictionary, *A Table Alphabeticall* (1604). His life was apparently so colourless that it did not merit an entry in the original edition of the *Dictionary of National Biography*. Nevertheless, his dictionary was recognized as a landmark text: as the first monolingual English dictionary, the start of a progression that led through Dr Johnson, Noah Webster, the *Oxford English Dictionary*, up to the English dictionaries of today.

But Cawdrey was more than just the first person to publish a monolingual English dictionary. He was the central character in a legal 'case' (stemming from his 'degradation' or expulsion from the clergy) which was one of the more important issues to come before the Star Chamber in the sixteenth century. The story of 'Cawdrey's case' was retailed in legal histories throughout the seventeenth and eighteenth centuries.

Recently the stories of Cawdrey the lexicographer and Cawdrey the defendant in the celebrated case have started to be pieced together, and a composite picture begins to emerge. The 2,500 or so entries in the first edition of Cawdrey's *Table Alphabeticall*, reproduced here from the only known copy, in the Bodleian Library in Oxford, are a significant part of that picture.

But we must begin at the beginning...

Cawdrey's early life

Robert Cawdrey is said to have been born in 1537 or 1538, towards the end of the reign of King Henry VIII. No official record of his birth has been found, so we know neither his place of birth nor the names of his parents. He probably grew up in the Midlands. Working back from later information, we find him teaching at 'the Grammer Schoole at Okeham' (Oakham) in Rutland around 1563. It seems that he did not attend university, but was nevertheless drawn to the Church. His teaching at Oakham continued until around 1571, but while teaching at the school he was ordained deacon in 1565 and then priest in 1570.

> **deacon,** prouider for the poore

His ability clearly impressed William Cecil, from 1571 the first Lord Burghley and one of Queen Elizabeth I's principal ministers and administrators. Burghley appointed Cawdrey in 1571 to the living of South Luffenham in Rutland, and Cawdrey was fortunate enough to benefit from his patronage and support for many years to come.

> **aduousion,** patronage, or power to present, or giue a liuing.

By now things appeared to be going rather well for Cawdrey. About this time he was married (and again, frustratingly, the relevant parish records appear to be lost and so we do not know the date of his marriage or the name of his wife). We do know, however, that he and his wife had eight children (five sons and three daughters). His son Thomas, who assisted him later with his dictionary, was born around 1575.

However, Cawdrey's fortunes were about to take a tumble, largely of his own making, and much of his life for the following two decades was to be coloured by the 'case' which dominated so much of his life at the time.

Cawdrey the Puritan

As a priest, Cawdrey was a nonconformist, a Puritan, and this soon led him into conflict with the established authorities. As early as 1576, five years after being instituted rector of South Luffenham, he ran into trouble with the church establishment for not reading homilies in church.

Things went from bad to worse. The ecclesiastical historian John Strype, writing in 1701 (in his *Historical collections of the life and acts of the Right Reverend Father in God, John Aylmer, Lord Bishop of London in the reign of Queen Elizabeth*), documents some of the accusations that were to be laid against Cawdrey over the next few years:

> There was preferred secretly an Information against him for speaking divers Words in the Pulpit, tending to the depraving of the Book of Common Prayer.[1]

In addition, he was accused of 'not Conforming himself in the Celebration of the Divine Service, and Administration of the Sacraments, but refusing to do so. Tho' indeed for the most Part he did Conform himself to the Book; only leaving out the Cross in Baptism, and the Ring in Marriage.'[2]

baptisme, dipping, or sprinkling.

He took his task as a preacher very seriously, and spoke later on of the importance of the preacher's role in the community. He regarded the role of village priest as much more important to the life of a community than the guidance offered by the higher orders of the church (the bishops and archbishops). In 1580 he sought a wider audience, publishing his first book, *A shorte and fruitefull treatise, of the profite and necessitie of catechising: that is of instructing the youth, and ignorant persons in the principles and groundes of Christian religion.* His wish to preach and instruct was carried forward in later years into his lexicography.

But despite his apparent self-confidence, his uncompromising attitude towards his religion and his duties as a parish priest was too extreme for the authorities. In 1586 he was recorded as arguing from the pulpit against the bishops for the equality of Christian ministers.

bishop, ouer-seer, or prelate.

In 1587 the Puritan Cawdrey was ordered to appear before the Court of High Commission, presided over by John Aylmer, the

Bishop of London, to answer the accusations made against him. It does not seem that Cawdrey endeared himself to his judges and as a result of the hearing Cawdrey was deprived of his living.

'He attended Ten Weeks upon the Commissioners. But proved altogether incompliant. And so being judged a dangerous Person, if he should continue preaching, by infecting the People with Principles different from the Religion established', Bishop Aylmer 'beside his Deprivation suspended him from exercising any Ministry in Luffenham or elsewhere'.[3] 'He was convicted upon his own Confession, publicly in his Sermon to have depraved the Book of Common-Prayer, Saying, That the same was a *Vile Book* and *Fy upon it*'.[4] Subsequent historians have seen Cawdrey's case as a milestone on the road to the creation of the Fifth Amendment of the American Constitution, which rules that no person 'shall be compelled in any criminal case to be a witness against himself'.

> **racha,** fie, a note of extreame anger, signified by the gesture of the person that speaketh it, to him that he speaketh to.

Cawdrey did not take this lying down. According to Strype 'he still kept possession and held the Living, stiling himself in his Letters Minister and Pastor of South Luffenham'.[5]

None of Cawdrey's actions were particularly unusual amongst Puritans at the time. But he was not prepared to accept his treatment under the Court of High Commission, and in 1590, in exasperation at being deprived of his living, he brought an action against the new chaplain of South Luffenham for 'trespass' on church property (taking corn from the church's glebe land) which he still regarded as part of his own living. This was something of a test case. The court produced a 'special verdict',[6] saying that on the facts of the case there was no doubt that Cawdrey was in the right and that trespass had occurred, but that if Cawdrey had previously been lawfully deprived of his living, as the Church maintained, then his claim failed. Cawdrey held that the earlier deprivation had been invalid under ecclesiastical law.

disgrade, to discharge of his orders, or degrees.

Throughout this time his family had been growing. Daniel, who became a rigorous Presbyterian and subsequently suffered many of the setbacks that his father encountered, was born in 1587 or 1588. Four of his sons (Anthony, Zachary, Daniel, and Thomas) would go on to study at Cambridge. But Cawdrey's clashes with the ec-clesiastical authorities made life at home hard, with little money, a large family, and (between 1587 and 1591) the constant threat of legal retribution.

ecclesiasticall, belonging to the church

The Star Chamber met in June 1591 to decide whether the earlier sentence of deprivation on Cawdrey was valid. Details of the case may be found in Sir Edward Coke's *Reports* (1612), where – unusually – the case was not listed under the name of the defendant, but was discussed under the general heading 'Of the Kings Ecclesiasticall Law' and was the prominent opening case in Part Five of the *Reports*. The case had rested on whether the earlier ecclesiastical court should have proceeded according to ecclesiastical law in a case which involved statute law. Cawdrey's side argued strongly, point for point, against their opponents. Letters flew between the various parties, Cawdrey's patron Lord Burghley attempting to make him agree to conform to the wishes of the Church. But although at times appearing ready to back down, in the end Cawdrey held his ground, and the Court confirmed the original sentences of deprivation of benefice and degradation from the priesthood.

recantation, an vnsaying of that which was said before

John Strype finishes, rather exasperatedly: 'And thus, at last this long Process seemed to be ended, (at least I know no more of it) which was in hand four Years and seven Months, and cost Cawdrey one or two and Twenty Journeys to London. The last Particular I meet with in this tedious suit, was, that the aforesaid Noble man [i.e. Lord Burghley] requested that this Man might be restored to the Ministry. Which Dr Lewin and Dr. Aubrey acquainted the Archbishop with. Who answered he was willing to do it, if he would subscribe to certain Articles, as other Ministers did. Which had been offered to him several Times before both by the Archbishop and the Bishop of London. But that Cawdrey would not be brought to do: neither could the Advice of his said Noble Intercessor prevail with him.'[7]

prolixe, tedious, long, or large.

Life after the Church

Cawdrey had come to the end of the road as far as his life within the established Church was concerned. As a result of his Puritanical zeal and his obstinacy he was left with a large family and no regular employment. It is likely that at this time he occupied himself with private teaching and preaching, and with writing.

The Dedication to his dictionary in 1604 says that many of its words were collected many years earlier. We can assume, then, that the idea of the dictionary developed as his relationship with the established Church waned. But his religious work continued in the background, and in 1598 he published his second instructional book, *A godlie forme of householde gouernment for the ordering of priuate families, according to the direction of Gods word. Whereunto is adjoyned in a more particular manner, the seuerall duties of the husband towards the wife: and the wifes dutie towards her husband. The Parents dutie towards their children, and the childrens towards the parents. The masters dutie towards his seruants: and also the seruants dutie towards their masters.* The full title perhaps shows the organized and uncompromising manner in which Cawdrey approached problems.

He spent much of his time now on writing projects. A revised edition of the *Godlie forme of householde gouernment* was published in 1600, and in the same year he published his third book, *A treasurie or store-house of similies both pleasaunt, delightfull, and profitable, for all estates of men in generall. Newly collected into heades and common places.* The next year, 1601, saw a revised edition of his first book, the *Shorte and fruitefull treatise,* originally published in 1580. There is little contemporary evidence for any celebrity attaching to Cawdrey at this time, though the fact that he is mentioned in passing in one of the scurrilous Marprelate Tracts, of 20 February 1589, indicates that his name was known: 'That the surplice is her Majesty's badge and cognisance: the defendant in this point, is father John Mar-elm, in Mr. Cawdrey's examination.'[8] 'John Mar-elm' was John Elmar (or Aylmer), the Bishop of London who had examined Cawdrey's case.

Cawdrey the lexicographer

Cawdrey's former life as a village priest had taught him the importance of plain English. His preaching was not directed towards a bookish audience, but towards the ordinary people who constituted his flock. He tells us in the Dedication to his dictionary (1604) that the words in his dictionary were collected 'long ago for the most part', presumably during or soon after his preaching days, and 'lately augmented by my sonne *Thomas,* who is now a School-maister in London'.

The period over which Cawdrey's words were collected was a significant one for the English language, and it is possible to see why a bookseller might decide that publishing such a book might be a worthwhile undertaking. England had gradually been developing a sense of national self-confidence throughout the reign of Elizabeth I, and with this self-confidence came a pride in the language. Cawdrey lived in the age of Shakespeare, Nashe, Spenser, Sidney, and many other literary giants, and the great works of literature, religion, law, history, exploration, and more were available to an increasingly literate and educated public.

The English language itself was developing rapidly at the time, too. According to statistics derived from the *Oxford English Dictionary* the late sixteenth century saw a peak in neologisms, as words flooded into English from other languages as a result of trade and exploration, and native coinages too increased in number as the language grew in strength.[9]

But what special qualities did Cawdrey have that caused him to become the first monolingual lexicographer in English? We have already seen that he was committed to simplicity in language, and that he was strong-minded to the point of obstinacy. He was already a published author, and had been active in the world of language use, as a preacher, for many years.

He states his purpose and audience on the title-page of his dictionary:

> A Table alphabeticall, conteyning and teaching the true writing,
> and understanding of hard vsuall English wordes, borrowed from
> the Hebrew, Greeke, Latine, or French, &c.

The dictionary, therefore, is not intended to be a complete record of contemporary English, but of 'hard usual' words from foreign languages. In fact the tradition of monolingual English dictionaries containing a broad sweep of the general language did not start to develop until the later years of the seventeenth century. Cawdrey continues:

> With the interpretation thereof by plaine English words, gath-
> ered for the benefit & helpe of Ladies, Gentlewomen, or any
> other vnskilfull persons.
>
> ✤

This statement of his intended audience is widely cited. What is less frequently referred to is his next sentence:

> Whereby they may the more easilie and better vnderstand many
> hard English wordes, which they shall heare or read in Scriptures,
> Sermons, or elswhere, and also be made able to vse the same aptly
> themselues.

(NB the two variant spellings of 'words' – 'wordes' and then 'words' – that he uses within a sentence of each other!)

Cawdrey therefore refers to the world of religion and preaching on the title-page of his work, and we shall see later that these aspects of his former life have an influence of his selection of vocabulary.

As with all dictionaries, the introductory text repays further reading. Some of it is derivative, but the argument of 'To the Reader' (where again 'Preachers' are mentioned in line two) is memorable for Cawdrey's inveighing against those who strive after ornate or complex language. He observes, perhaps rather harshly (but echoing a commonplace of the time), that 'some men seek so far for outlandish English, that they forget altogether their mothers language, so that if some of their mothers were aliue, they were not able to tell, or vnderstand what they say.'

The introductory essay ends, curiously to a modern reader, with instructions on how to find a word in the dictionary. 'Nowe if the word, which thou art desirous to finde, begin with (a) then looke in the beginning of this Table, but if with (v) looke towards the end [etc.].' Nevertheless, problems occur on the very first page of the dictionary, where the entry for *aberration* is repeated at *abb-* and *abe-*!

Before we look in some detail at Cawdrey's lexicographical method we should examine the correctness of the claim that Cawdrey's is the first English dictionary. The title of Gabriele Stein's book *The English Dictionary before Cawdrey* (1985) suggests that there is more to the question than meets the eye.

Cawdrey did not invent lexicography in English. His work was preceded by several bilingual dictionaries (Latin-English, French-English, Italian-English, etc.), by word-lists included in or attached to other works, and by specialist monolingual glossaries (especially in the law). As we have seen, his dictionary does not seek to cover the whole of the language, but is restricted to 'hard usual words'. As far as is known, it is the first dictionary published in book form addressed to the general reader which defines 'usual' English words in English. His work was preceded abroad by equivalent monolingual dictionaries of several of the continental languages. Cawdrey has the pre-eminent claim to be regarded as the compiler of the first monolingual English dictionary.

A review of related texts published before the *Table Alphabeticall* shows that Cawdrey was incorporating facts and ideas which were generally available to scholars at the time. Several things, however, stand out. Firstly, Cawdrey's text was the first to be published in book form in England. This implies that he or his publisher had identified a gap in the market which they hoped to fill. The time was ripe, or even overripe, for a monolingual dictionary, and Cawdrey was astute enough to seize this opportunity.

Secondly, Cawdrey – as other great lexicographers after him – took existing ideas and created something new out of them. His lexicographical style moved dictionary-writing forward, and opened up a discipline which others could develop.

Thirdly, Cawdrey seems to have had something of an agenda behind his lexicography. His dictionary can be seen as more than just a list of words and definitions designed to aid the 'vnskilfull'.

Amongst the earlier texts of which Cawdrey made use was a book by another schoolmaster, Edmund Coote, which was published in 1596. Coote was at the time of its publication a schoolmaster seventy miles away from Cawdrey, in Bury St Edmunds, though he later had to move schools for reasons that have not been discovered. There is no evidence that the two men knew each other. Coote's book contains advice to scholars on grammar, spelling, and other schoolmasterly topics. It also (in a manner that may have endeared him to Cawdrey) contains a catechism and copies of numerous psalms for use in school. Furthermore, it also contains a fairly extensive glossary, which attempts in particular to help scholars appreciate the difference between English words deriving from Latin, Greek, and French. Coote precedes his glossary with 'Directions for the vnskilfull',[10] including the information about the location of letters within the alphabet that Cawdrey copied closely in his own introduction.

Two further points, at least, are worthy of note. Firstly, Coote uses a very similar selection of typefaces to Cawdrey. Headwords are presented in a roman fount, and the glosses or definitions are presented in black letter.

Secondly, Cawdrey makes use of a large number of Coote's headwords. Coote's first two entries run:

> **Abandon** cast away.
> **abba** father.

Cawdrey's dictionary opens with the following:

> **Abandon,** cast away, or yeelde vp, to leaue, or forsake.
> **Abash,** blush.
> **Abba,** father.

A comparison of the equivalent stretch of entries from *morality* to *mystery* in both dictionaries shows that Cawdrey borrows thirteen of Coote's headwords, omitting only *mountaine* as presumably not 'hard' enough for his readers. Furthermore, Cawdrey typically uses Coote's glosses as the bases for his own definitions:

> **motiue,** cause moouing, or the thyng, and reason, that mooueth to doe any thing. [Coote: 'cause mouing'.]

> **mortifie,** kill, or make dead, and senselesse. [Coote: 'kill'.]

On first glance, in fact, the two texts look remarkably similar in form and content.

Coote was not Cawdrey's only source. Recent work on Cawdrey has shown that he appears to have made his selection of headwords from a number of sources, including legal glossaries, bilingual dictionaries (particularly Thomas Thomas's Latin-English dictionary of 1587), and several other works. Thomas's dictionary was itself dedicated to Lord Burghley, Cawdrey's patron. Of his eleven additions to Coote in the range from *morality* to *mystery* Cawdrey seems to have taken six from Thomas, perhaps one from John Rastell's *Exposition of certaine difficult and obscure words, and terms of the lawes of this realme* (maybe from the 1602 edition), and several from other sources.

Cawdrey's purpose was not to be original in his selection, but to instruct using the most appropriate terms. His skill lies in adapting his definitions to his audience. A detailed examination of Cawdrey's style may be found in Ray Siemens's 'Lexicographical Method in Cawdrey', using computational aids to examine the content of Cawdrey's first and subsequent editions. While noting Cawdrey's borrowing of headwords, Siemens continues to analyse the stylistic structures in Cawdrey's definitions by part of speech. He concludes that 'the majority of Cawdrey's definitions…, simple and complex alike, adhere to relatively set structures following the syntactic categories of their headword. Much as might be expected, nouns are generally defined by one or more noun phrases, and at times with a verb phrase. Definitions of verbs most commonly contain a series of verb phrases, sometimes joined with a preposition and noun phrase. Adjectives are defined either by synonym(s) or with noun and verb phrases.'[11] The reader of this volume can judge the accuracy of this by consulting Cawdrey's definitions themselves.

In terms of structure, we can see Cawdrey moving towards standardization. He is not entirely successful, but the structure he imposes on his text is of a higher nature than that found in his sources. He has a weak point, and that is punctuation. There seems to be no rationale in whether he chooses to end a definition with a full stop, a semi-colon, or with nothing.

Beyond that, he is fairly consistent in his alphabetical ordering of headwords (at least to the extent that we can be sure that he intends to be alphabetical). He introduces headwords with a lower-case letter (in contrast to many subsequent dictionaries, but in keeping with modern practice). He offers a single definitive headword spelling, and is reasonably consistent about the spelling when these words themselves occur within definitions. He normally uses the base or infinitive form of a word as his headword (though occasionally allows a plural noun as a headword).

His entries are, as he states, principally for words which he considers to derive from Latin, Greek, French, and Hebrew. He does not seek to include terms of Germanic origin. His interpretation of the complex issues of etymology is somewhat simplistic. Coote offers better advice (on the basis of knowledge at that time) on ways to distinguish between words from these sources. In keeping with other similar texts from the seventeenth century Cawdrey does not provide etymological information (other than a letter or symbol indicating the language of origin if he does not derive it from Latin), and he does not use the square brackets which subsequently became the traditional means of marking out etymologies, though these have been supplied in the present edition. He does not indicate parts of speech for his headwords, nor does he provide any attempt at a representation of their pronunciation. But we would not expect that at this time.

The extensions he offers to the definitions of his predecessors show a keen awareness of his audience. When his source is abrupt, he often adds a phrase which provides more context for his reader, as with:

> **alphabet,** order of letters in the crosse-row. [Cf. Coote: 'order
> of letters'; the 'cross-row' was so called from the symbol
> of the Cross which preceded the alphabet in horn-books
> of the period.]

> **obscure,** darke, or cloudie [Coote: 'darke'.]

He shows an awareness of the need to define in terms which his reader may understand, rather than simply to provide an equivalent gloss (which may be ambiguous).

Perhaps the most intriguing aspect of Cawdrey's little book relates to its purpose. Did Cawdrey have a hidden agenda in selecting his vocabulary and presenting his entries in a style which could be understood readily by his audience?

Sylvia Brown has written persuasively on Cawdrey's employment of rhetoric, with special emphasis on his female readers (as highlighted on the title-page of his dictionary). She sees a development from his religious works to his dictionary. '[Cawdrey] is suggesting that his dictionary originates in and for a godly community; the understanding which Cawdrey seeks to promote will be of service to – and will indeed produce – 'godlie' readers.'[12] Without attempting to present a general theory, I think it is quite possible to examine Cawdrey's selection of vocabulary for his dictionary and to find indications of a similar purpose.

We have seen that Cawdrey was building on earlier lexicographical work in compiling his dictionary. He took styles and words from a number of sources, and amalgamated them into a new form, the dictionary of English as a published book.

A review of his entries in the part of the letter 'M' (*moral – mystery*) shows that the words he took from Coote's *English Schoolemaister* were predominantly words which entered English (according to the *Oxford English Dictionary*) in the Middle Ages. This might be expected from a text which concentrates on words from Latin, Greek, and French. But the other words which Cawdrey added to his dictionary often date from the sixteenth century, and were sometimes quite recent additions to the language. He shows an awareness of the emergent vocabulary of his time, as one might expect of a lexicographer.

The *Oxford English Dictionary* contains about 60,000 headwords for words which were current in 1600, of which Cawdrey selected only 2,500. Of those he might have chosen from the latter part of 'M' (835 headwords in the *OED*) he has excluded many that might have fallen within his remit (*morbid, mordant, mortmain, mosaic,* etc.). We should probably assume that he was unable to include as many words as he might have liked, in order to keep his book within bounds. It was, after all, an exploratory venture.

Despite this, it becomes apparent as one reads through his text that his original intention of presenting a text which assists in the understanding of 'Scriptures' and 'Sermons' seems to affect his choice of headwords. There are occasionally entries for everyday items and, more frequently, entries for plants and animals (though these appear to have been entered unsystematically). 'Crocodile' stands out. He defines this as '[a kind of] beast', somewhat unhelpfully for someone whose job it is to clarify meaning. The entry seems to be present simply as a guide to spelling. But there is no entry for 'elephant', which presumably offered his audience similar problems. Other sets of words which appear throughout the dictionary are terms concerned with the law, the heavens, and rhetoric.

Ray Siemens provides information on the entries Cawdrey includes by part of speech. Nouns predominate, as one might expect, comprising half the total wordlist. The other entries are more or less equally split between adjectives and verbs, with a small number of entries for words from other parts of speech.[13]

There are in fact rather more adjectives and nouns than might be expected in a dictionary of the period. This is perhaps because Cawdrey wished to include terms which had a moral slant, and indeed it is noticeable in some parts of the dictionary that whole ranges of his selected headwords have (or can be interpreted as having) such an edge. They are often words which the lay reader might come across in religious texts, and especially in commentaries of religion, such as sermons: the letter 'H' includes *halaluiah, hallucinate, hautie, heathen, hebrew, hecticke, heretecall, hermite, heroicall, hideous, hymne, hipocrite, homage, homicide, horror, hosanna, hospitality, hostage, hostilitie, huckster,* and *humane* among its 46 entries. The close of 'U/V' includes, in quick succession, *vicious, vigilance, vigour, vincible, violate, violent, viperine, virago, virulent, vision, vitall, vitiate, viuificent, viuifie, vlcer,* and *vlcerate.* This is not to say that the dictionary is swamped with terms which have a moral edge, but enough exist to substantiate a suggestion that Cawdrey has a religious agenda.

Tom Webster has drawn attention to Cawdrey's definition of the term 'conference' ('communication, talking together') as one which has resonance with the meetings of Puritan ministers under Charles I, who would often arrange 'Christian conferences' before chosen godly ministers as a means of addressing doctrinal disputes amongst themselves, rather than involving the ecclesiastical authorities (who would be inclined to fine them or worse).[14]

The counterpart in the Elizabethan church was the presbyterian classis, which involved the ministers of a county meeting together (of necessity, secretly) in order to resolve questions of doctrine and discipline; this was intended to challenge the episcopacy. Was Cawdrey, in including the term 'conference' in his dictionary, perhaps signalling at least his awareness of and possibly his sympathy for the underground presbyterian movement of his time?

Another way of examining this issue is by looking at those entries in Cawdrey's dictionary which the *Oxford English Dictionary* cites as the first recorded occurrence of a word. Of Cawdrey's 2,500 entries, the second edition of the *OED* (1989) regards 31 as first occurrences in English. As work continues on the third edition of the *OED* this number has dropped to 26, and will doubtless fall further as editorial work progresses. One of the *OED*'s quotations (*nauseous*) had been wrongly dated from the first edition of Cawdrey, when it actually occurred first in a later edition. Of the other four earlier uses, all come from texts which have a religious connection: two come from James I's *Daemonologie* (1597)(*manic* and *peccant*), a discourse on witchcraft; one derives from a Scottish ecclesiastical register (*option*); and the last (*omniscient*) is predated by Francis Meres's translation of Father Luis de Granada's *Sinners Guyde* (1598).

The evidence of Cawdrey's dictionary, therefore, seems to show that throughout his life he remained dedicated to bringing both an educational and a Christian message to his audience, both in his church work and in his lexicography. As a side-effect, he opened up a new branch of publishing in England, that of the monolingual English dictionary.

Cawdrey's life after the dictionary

The last certainty we know about Cawdrey is that he signed the dedicatory epistle to his dictionary on 27 June 1604, in Coventry. It is assumed that he died quite soon after, but this is purely specula-tion. His dictionary continued into three further editions (in 1609, 1613, and 1617), gradually expanding its wordlist with each edition. There is no evidence that Cawdrey was involved in any of the later editions. The edition of 1609 was 'newly corrected and much in-larged' by his son Thomas, who had himself published a derivative grammatical text (*The examination of the accidence by qvestions and answeres*) in 1606. Thomas subsequently left schoolmastering to become a doctor, qualifying as a Doctor of Medicine in 1611. The third edition of Cawdrey's dictionary (1613) was 'set forth by R.C. and newly corrected, and much inlarged with many words now in vse', presumably by another hand. In 1612 Cawdrey's *Godlie forme of householde gouernment* was also in new hands ('first gathered by R.C.; and now newly perused, amended, and augmented, by Iohn Dod, and Robert Cleuer').

Of his other sons, Zachary married Ann Withers in Melton Mowbray, Leicestershire in 1617 (there are also marriage records of a Zachary Cawdrey in Leicestershire in 1604 and again in 1606). Zachary's own son Zachary (1618–84) was a clergyman and author. *The Oxford Dictionary of National Biography* ends its article on Zachary Cawdrey the younger with a quotation which is oddly reminiscent of his grandfather Robert: Zachary was 'a conformist, and formerly a great sufferer for the King, but in his latter times much maligned and reproached by some people for his moderation towards dissenters'.[15]

Cawdrey's son Daniel (1587/8–1664) is also the subject of an extensive 'life' in the *Oxford Dictionary of National Biography*. After graduating from Cambridge, he was ordained priest in 1614 and gained the living of Great Ilford in Essex and subsequently that of Great Billing in Northamptonshire. As a leading nonconformist, he had an eventful career, publishing a number of religious texts, before being ejected from Great Billing in 1662. He seems to have married Katherine Cleere in 1617, and to have had at least two children. Of Cawdrey's son Anthony nothing seems to be known, unless he is the Anthony Cawdrey who was married to an Anne Jessop at Ropesley in Lincolnshire in September 1610.

Conclusion

Robert Cawdrey's career in the church and as a lexicographer was for many years shrouded in mystery. His dictionary has long been celebrated as the first monolingual dictionary of English, but the facts of Cawdrey's life as they have gradually been pieced together in recent years show that Cawdrey's dictionary and his religious work are interwoven. The publication of John Bullokar's *English Expositor: teaching the interpretation of the hardest words used in our language* in 1616 seems to have sounded the death knell for the popularity of Cawdrey's work, as others moved into this area of publishing and the monolingual English dictionary became to claim a place on the bookshelves of the nation. John Bullokar in 1616 did not mention his immediate predecessor Cawdrey, and Elisha Coles, whose dictionary appeared some sixty years later, states that he is not 'ignorant of what's already done. I know the whole Succession from Dr. Bullokar to Dr. Skinner'.[16] Cawdrey's dictionary did not, it seems, bring him international fame during his lifetime or in the years following his death. But the appearance in 1604 of a little book containing definitions of some of the 'hard usual' words of the English language marks a turning point in English lexicography and paves the way for some of the most remarkable reference books that have been produced in the English language.

Notes

1   John Strype, *Historical collections of the life and acts of the Right Reverend Father in God, John Aylmer...* (London, 1701), p. 129.

2   Ibid., p. 130.

3   Ibid., pp. 129–130.

4   Ibid., p. 134.

5   Ibid., p. 130.

6   Sir Edward Coke, *The fift part of the reports of Sr. Eduuard Coke knight...,* (London, 1612), f. 1/2.

7   Strype, *Historical collections,* pp. 147–8.

8   Martin Marprelate, *Certaine minerall, and metaphisicall schoolpoints to be defended by the reuerende bishops* (Coventry, 1589).

9   Charlotte Brewer, *Examining the OED,* Initial results/Outline material/OED quotations per decade 1500–1899 <http://oed.hertford.ox.ac.uk/main/content/view/45/124/>, accessed 13 August 2006.

10 Edmund Coote, *The English schoole-maister: teaching all his scholers, the order of distinct reading, and true writing our English tongue* (London, 1596), p. 72.

11 Raymond Siemens, *The Acorn of the Oak: A Stylistic Approach to Lexicographical Method in Cawdrey's* A Table Alphabeticall <http://www.chass.utoronto.ca/epc/chwp/siemens1/siem5.html>, accessed 13 August 2006.

12 Silvia Brown, 'Women and the Godly Art of Rhetoric: Robert Cawdrey's Puritan Dictionary', *Studies in English Literature 1500–1900* 41, 1 (2001), 133–148, (p. 141).

13 Siemens, *The Acorn of the Oak,* <www.chass.utoronto.ca/epc/chwp/siemens1/siem4.html>.

14 Tom Webster, *Godly clergy in early Stuart England: the Caroline Puritan movement* (Cambridge, 1977), p. 57.

15 S. J. Guscott, 'Cawdrey , Zachary (1618–1684)', *Oxford Dictionary of National Biography* (Oxford, 2004) <http://www.oxforddnb. com/view/article/4956>, accessed 13 August 2006.

16 Elisha Coles, *An English dictionary explaining the difficult terms that are used in Divinity, Husbandry, Physick, Phylosophy, Law, Navigation, Mathematics, and other arts and sciences* (London, 1676), 'To the reader'.

Bibliography and Further Reading

Bately, Janet, 'Cawdrey, Robert', *Oxford Dictionary of National Biography* (Oxford, 2004) <http://www.oxforddnb.com/view/article/69578>, accessed 13 August 2006.

Brown, Sylvia, 'Women and the Godly Art of Rhetoric: Robert Cawdrey's Puritan Dictionary', *Studies in English Literature 1500–1900* 41, 1 (2001), 133–148.

Brewer, Charlotte, *Examining the OED*, Initial results/Outline material/OED quotations per decade 1500-1899, <http://oed.hertford.ox.ac.uk/main/ content/ view/45/124/>, accessed 13 August 2006.

Coke, Sir Edward, *The fift part of the reports of Sr. Eduuard Coke knight, the Kings attorney generall: of diuers resolutions and iudgments giuen vpon great deliberation, in matters of great importance & consequence by the reuerend iudges and sages of the law: together with the reasons and causes of their resolutions and iudgements* (London, 1612).

Coles, Elisha, *An English dictionary: explaining the difficult terms that are used in Divinity, Husbandry, Physick, Phylosophy, Law, Navigation, Mathematics, and other arts and sciences* (London, 1676).

Coote, Edmund, *The English schoole-maister: teaching all his scholers, the order of distinct reading, and true writing our English tongue* (London, 1596).

Guscott, S. J.,'Cawdrey, Zachary (1618–1684)', *Oxford Dictionary of National Biography* (Oxford, 2004) <http://www.oxforddnb.com/view/article/4956>, accessed 13 August 2006.

Lancashire, Ian, 'Law and Early Modern English Lexicons', *Selected Proceedings of the 2005 Symposium on New Approaches in English Historical Lexis (HEL-LEX)*, ed. R. W. McConchie *et al.*, 8–23 (Somerville, MA., 2006).

['Marprelate, Martin'], *Certaine minerall, and metaphisicall schoolpoints to be defended by the reuerende bishops* (Coventry, 1589).

OED Online <http://dictionary.oed.com> (Oxford, 2006), accessed 13 August 2006.

Rastell, John, *An Exposition of certaine difficult and obscure words, and Termes of the Lawes of this Realme. Newly amended and augmented, both in French and English, for the help of such young students as are desirous to attaine to the knowledge of the same* (London, 1602) [First edn. c.1523].

Schäfer, Jürgen, *A Survey of Monological Printed Glossaries and Dictionaries 1475–1640, Vol. 1: Early Modern English Lexicography* (Oxford, 1989).

Siemens, Raymond, *The Acorn of the Oak: A Stylistic Approach to Lexicographical Method in Cawdrey's* A Table Alphabeticall (1996) <http://www.chass.utoronto.ca/epc/chwp/siemens1/>, accessed 13 August 2006.

Starnes, De Witt T. and Noyes, Gertrude E., *The English dictionary from Cawdrey to Johnson, 1604–1755; new edition with an introduction and a selected bibliography by Gabriele Stein* (Amsterdam, 1991).

Stein, Gabriele, *The English dictionary before Cawdrey* (Tübingen, 1985).

Strype, John, *Historical collections of the life and acts of the Right Reverend Father in God, John Aylmer, Lord Bishop of London in the reign of Queen Elizabeth* (London, 1701).

Thomas, Thomas, *Dictionarium linguae Latinae et Anglicanae* (London, 1587).

Webster, Tom, *Godly clergy in early Stuart England: the Caroline Puritan movement* (Cambridge, 1977).

DICTIONARY

A Note on the Text

The spelling and punctuation of the 1604 edition have been retained with two exceptions. Abbreviated words have been expanded. In addition, Cawdrey uses the following abbreviations:

(k) standeth for a kind of.
(g. or gr.) standeth for Greeke.
The French words haue this (§) before them.

For ease of reading, this edition uses the modern convention of square brackets. Thus, (k) is printed [k], (g. and gr.) as [gr], and (§) is substituted by [fr].

A Table Alphabeticall, conteyning and teaching the
true writing, and vnderstanding of hard vsuall English
wordes, borrowed from the Hebrew, Greeke, Latine, or
French. &c.

With the interpretation thereof by *plaine English
words, gathered for the benefit & helpe of Ladies, Gentlewomen, or any other vnskilfull persons.*

Whereby they may the more easilie and better
vnderstand many hard English wordes, which
they shall heare or read in Scriptures, Sermons, or
elswhere, and also be made able to vse the same aptly
themselues.

Legere, et non intelligere, neglegere est.
As good not read, as not to vnderstand.

AT LONDON, Printed by I. R. for Edmund Weauer,
& are to be sold at his shop at the great North doore of
Paules Church. 1604.

CRO

To the right honourable, Worshipfull, vertuous, &
godlie Ladies, the Lady Hastings, the Lady Dudley,
the Lady Mountague, the Ladie Wingfield, and the
Lady Leigh, his Christian friends, R. C. wisheth great
prosperitie in this life, with increase of grace, and peace
from GOD our Father, through Iesus Christ our Lord
and onely Sauiour.

*BY this Table (right Honourable & Worshipfull) strangers that blame
our tongue of difficultie, and vncertaintie, may heereby plainly see, &
better vnderstand those things, which they haue thought hard. Heerby
also the true Orthography, that is, the true writing of many hard
English words, borrowed from the Greeke, Latine & French, and how
to know one from the other, with the interpretation thereof by plaine
English words, may be learned and knowne. And children heere by
may be prepared for the vnderstanding of a great number of Latine
words: which also will bring much delight & iudgement to others, by
the vse of this little worke. Which worke, long ago for the most part,
was gathered by me, but lately augmented by my sonne* Thomas, *who
now is Schoolemaister in London.*

The Epistle.

Now when I had called to mind (right honorable and Worshipfull) the great kindnesse, and bountifulnes, which I found in that vertuous & godly Lady, Lucie Harington, *your Honours and Worships mother, and my especiall friend in the Lord. When, and at such time as the right Worshipfull* Sir Iames Harington *Knight, your Ladiships brother was my scholler, (and now my singuler benefactor) when I taught the Grammer schoole at Okeham in the County of* Rutland: *In consideration whereof, and also for that I acknowledge my selfe much beholding and indebted to the most of you, since this time, (beeing all naturall sisters) I am bold to make you all ioyntly patrons heereof, and vnder your names to publish this simple worke. And thus praying, that God of his vnspeakeable mercies, will blesse both your Honors and Worships, I doe with all good wishes to you all, with all yours, as to mine owne soule, humbly take my leaue. Couentry this xxvij. of Iune. 1604.*

Your Honors and Worships,

euer ready in Christ Iesus

to be commaunded, *Robert Cawdrey.*

To the Reader.

SVch as by their place and calling, (but especially Preachers) as haue occasion to speak publiquely before the ignorant people, are to bee admonished, that they neuer affect any strange ynckhorne termes, but labour to speake so as is commonly receiued, and so as the most ignorant may well vnderstand them: neyther seeking to be ouer fine or curious, nor yet liuing ouer carelesse, vsing their speech, as most men doe, & ordering their wits, as the fewest haue done. Some men seek so far for outlandish English, that they forget altogether their mothers language, so that if some of their mothers were aliue, they were not able to tell, or vnderstand what they say, and yet these fine English Clearks, will say they speak in their mother tongue; but one might well charge them, for counterfeyting the Kings English. Also, some far iournied gentlemen, at their returne home, like as they loue to go in forraine apparrell, so they will pouder their talke with ouer-sea language. He that commeth lately out of France, will talk French English, and neuer blush at the matter.

Another chops in with English Italianated, and applyeth the Italian phrase to our English speaking, the which is, as if an Orator, that professeth to vtter his minde in plaine Latine, would needs speake Poetrie, & far fetched colours of strange antiquitie. Doth any wise man think, that wit resteth in strange words, or els standeth it not in wholsome matter, and apt declaring of a mans mind? Do we not speak, because we would haue other to vnderstand vs?

or is not the tongue giuen for this end, that one might know what another meaneth? Therefore, either wee must make a difference of English, & say, some is learned English, & other-some is rude English, or the one is Court talke, the other is Country-speech, or els we must of necessitie banish all affected Rhetorique, and vse altogether one manner of language. Those therefore that will auoyde this follie, and acquaint themselues with the plainest & best kind of speech, must seeke from time to time such words as are commonlie receiued, and such as properly may expresse in plaine manner, the whole conceit of their mind. And looke what words wee best vnderstand, and know what they meane, the same should soonest be spoken, and first applied, to the vttrance of our purpose. Therfore for this end, foure things would chiefly be obserued in the choise of wordes. First, that such words as wee vse, should be proper vnto the tongue wherein we speake. Againe, that they be plaine for all men to perceiue. Thirdly, that they be apt and meete, most properly to set out the matter. Fourthlie, that words trans-lated, from one signification to another, (called of the Grecians *Tropes*,) be vsed to beautifie the sentence, as precious stones are set in a ring, to commend the gold. Now such are thought apt words, that properly agree vnto that thing, which they signifie, and plainly expresse the nature of the same. Therefore, they that haue regard of their estimation and credite, do warily speake, & with choise, vtter words most apt for their purpose. In waightie causes, graue wordes are thought most needfull, that the greatnes of the matter, may the rather appeare, in the vehemencie of theyr talke. So likewise of other, like order must be taken. Albeit some, not onely doe not obserue this kind of aptnesse, but also they fall into much fondnes, by vsing words out of place, and applying them to diuers matters, without all discretion.

If thou be desirous (gentle Reader) rightly and readily to vnderstand, and to profit by this Table, and such like, then thou must learne the Alphabet, to wit, the order of the Letters as they stand, perfecty without booke, and where euery Letter standeth: as (b) neere the beginning, (n) about the middest, and (t) toward the end. Nowe if the word, which thou art desirous to finde, begin with (a) then looke in the beginning of this Table, but if with (v) looke towards the end. Againe, if thy word beginne with (ca) looke in the beginning of the letter (c) but if with (cu) then looke toward the end of that letter. And so of all the rest. &c.

And further vnderstand, that whereas all such words as are deriued & drawne from the Greek, are noted with these letter, (g). And the French are marked thus (§) but such words as are deriued from the latin, haue no marke at all.

A Table Alphabeticall,

contayning and teaching the true
writing, and vnderstanding of hard
vsuall English words. &c.

(k) standeth for a kind of.
(g. or gr.) standeth for Greeke.
The French words haue this (§) before them.

A

ABandon, [fr] cast away, or yeelde vp, to leaue, or forsake.

Abash, blush.

abba, father.

abbesse, [fr] abbatesse, Mistris of a Nunnerie, comforters of others.

abbettors, [fr] counsellors.

aberration, a going a stray, or wandering.

abbreuiat,
abbridge [fr], } to shorten, or make short.

abbut, [fr] to lie vnto, or border vpon, as one lands end meets with another.

abecedarie, the order of the Letters, or hee that vseth them.

aberration, a going astray, or wandering.

abet, [fr] to maintaine.

abdicate, put away, refuse, or forsake.

abhorre, hate, despise, or disdaine.

abiect, base, cast away, in disdaine:

abiure, renounce, denie, forsweare:

abolish,
abolited, } make voyde, destroy, deface, or out of vse.

abortiue, [fr] borne before the time.

abricot, [k] kind of fruit:

abrogate, take away, disanull, disallow,

abruptly, vnorderly, without a preface.

absolue, finish, or acquite:

absolute, perfect, or vpright.

absolution, forgiuenes, discharge:

abstract, drawne away from another: a litbooke or volume
gathered out of a greater.

absurd, foolish, irksome.

academie, an Uniuersitie, as Cambridge, or Oxford:

academicke, of the sect of wise and learned men.

accent, tune, the rising or falling of the voice.

accept, to take liking of, or to entertaine willingly.

acceptance, [fr] an agreeing to some former act done before.

accesse, free comming to, or a way to a place,

accessarie, partaker in the same thing

accessorie, [fr] an accident extraordinary

accident, a chance, or happening.

accidentall, falling by chance, not by nature

accomodate, to make fit too, or conuenient to the purpose

a**ccomplish,** [fr] finish, or make an end of.

accommodating, lending

account, [fr] reckon.

accord, [fr] agreement betweene persons

accurate, curious, cunning, diligent.

accrew, [fr] grow, increase, goe.

acertaine, [fr] make sure, certifie.

acetositie, sharpnes, or sowernesse

acheeue, [fr] to make an end of

acquitall, [fr] discharge

acquisition, getting, purchasing

action, [fr] the forme of a suite

actiue, nimble, ready, quicke.

actuall, in act, or shewing it selfe in deed

acute, sharp, wittie, quick

adage, an old speech, or prouerbe,

adamantine, as hard as Diamont

addict, giuen too, appointed too

adhærent, cleauing to, or taking part with.

adiew, [fr] farewell

addresse, [fr] prepare, or direct.

adiacint, lying too, adioyning too

adiunct, an accidentall qualitie, or any property, that is not a
    substance.

adiourne, [fr] deferre, or put off till another time.

adiure, make to sweare, or to deny

administer, gouerne, serue, or rule, or doe seruice vnto

administrator, one that doth busines for an other

admire, maruell at, or be in loue with

admiration, wonderment, reioycing

admirall, [fr] chiefe by sea, worthy

admission, receiuing, or leaue to enter into a place, accept.

adopt, to take for his child, freely to choose

adore, [fr] worship, or reuerence,

adorne, beautifie, apparrell, prepare.

aduaunce, [fr] preferre, lift vp to honor:

aduent, the comming

aduerse, contrary, or backward

aduertise, [fr] giue knowledge, aduise, or counsell:

adulation, flatterie, or fauning

adulterate, to counterfeit, or corrupt:

aduocate, a spokesman, atturney, or man of law, plead.

aduousion, [fr] patronage, or power to present, or giue a liuing.

adustion, burning, or rosting.

Æ, see E.

affable, readie, and curteous in speech, gracious in words.

affaires, [fr] busines

affect, [fr] to desire earnestly, or to mind

affected, disposed, inclined

affinitie, kinne by marriage

affirme, auouch, acertaine

affiance, [fr] trust

affianced, [fr] betrothed

affranchise, [fr] set at libertie.

agent, dooer, a steward, or commissioner

aggrauate, make more grieuous, and more heauie:

agilitie, nimblenes, or quicknes

agglutinate, to ioyne together

agnition, knowledge, or acknowledging

agitate, driuen, stirred, tossed

agonie, [gr] heauie passion, anguish, griefe

aigre, [fr] sharpe, sower,

akecorne, [k] fruit

alacritie, cheerefulnes, liuelines

alablaster, [k] stone

alarum, a sound to the battell.

alchimie, the art of turning other mettals into gold.

alien, [fr] a stranger

alienate, [fr] to estrange, or with-drawe the mind, or to make a
    thing another mans.

all haile, salute

alledge, bring proofe

allegation, alledging

allegorie, [gr] similitude, a misticall speech, more then the bare
    letter

allegiance, [fr] obedience of a subiect

allienate, asswage, or make more easie and light

alliance, [fr] kindred, or league.

allusion, meaning and pointing to another matter then is spoken
    in words

allude, to speake one thing that hath resemblance and respect to
    another,

aliment, nourishment, sustenance

alpha, [gr] the first Greeke letter

alphabet, [gr] order of letters in the crosse-row.

altercation, debate, wrangling, or contention

altitude, height

amaritude, bitternesse

ambage, long circumstance of words.

ambassadour, [fr] messenger

ambition, desire of honour, or striuing for preferment

ambodexter, one that playeth on both hands.

ambiguous, doubtfull, vncertaine

ambushment, [fr] priuie traine, lying secretly to intrap by the way

amerce, [fr]
amercement, } fine, or penalty.

amiable, louely, or with a good grace.

amitie, friendship, loue.

amorous, full of loue, amiable.

amorte, [fr] dead, extinguished, without life.

amplifie, enlarge, or make bigger.

analogie, [gr] conuenience, proportion.

analisis, [gr] resolution, deuiding into parts.

anarchie, [gr] when the land is without a prince, or gouernour.

anatomie, [gr] cutting vp of the body.

anathema, [gr] accursed or giuen ouer to the deuill.

anchoue, [k] of fruite.

angle, [fr] corner.

anguish, [fr] griefe.

angust, straight, narrow.

animate, encourage.

animaduersion, noting, considering, or marking.

annalis, chronicles of things from yeare to yeare.

annex, to knit or ioyne together.

annihilate, make voyd, or bring to nothing.

anniuersarie, a yeares minde, or done and comming yearely.

annuall, yearely.

anthem, song.

antecessor, an auncestour, or predecessour that goeth or liueth in the age or place before vs.

antichrist, [gr] against, or contrarie to Christ.

anticipation, preuenting by a foreknowledge.

antidote, [gr] a counterpoise, or remedy against poyson.

antidate, [fr] a fore date.

antipathie, [gr] contrarietie of qualities.

antiquitie, auncientnes.

anticke, disguised.

antithesis, [gr] a repugnancie, or contrarietie.

antiquarie, a man skilled, or a searcher of antiquities.

annotations, briefe doctrines or instructions.

anxitie, care or sorrow.

aphorisme, [gr] generall rule in phisick.

apocalipse, [gr] reuelation.

apocrypha, [gr] not of authoritie, a thing hidden, whose originall is not knowne.

apologie, [gr] defence, or excuse by speech.

apostotate, [gr] a backslider.

apostacie, [gr] falling away, backslyding, rebellion.

apostle, [gr] an ambassadour, or one sent.

apothegme, [gr] short wittie sentence, or speech.

apparant, in sight, or open.

appall, feare.

apparition, appearance, or strange sight.

appeach, [fr] accuse, or bewray.

appeale, [fr] to seeke to a higher Iudge.

appease, [fr] quiet, or pacifie.

appendix, hanging, or belonging to another thing.

appertinent,
appurtenance, } belonging vnto another thing.

appetite, desire to any thing.

applaude, to shew a liking of, as it were by clapping of hands.

application, applying too, or resorting to

appose, to aske questions, oppose.

apposition, adding or setting too.

apprehension, conceite, and vnderstanding.

approbation, allowance, or liking.

appropriate, to take, and keepe to, and for himselfe alone.

approue, alowe, or make good.

approch, come nigh.

apt, fit.

arbiter,
arbitratour, } a Iudge in a controuersie betwixt men.

arbitrement, [fr] iudgement, censure, award.

arch, [gr] chiefe.

arch-angell, [gr] chiefe angell

archbishop, chiefe bishop

architest, chiefe builder.

ardent, hoate, earnest

ardencie, heate, earnestnes

argent, siluer, coyne

argue, to reason

ariditie, drinesse

aristocraticall, [gr] gouernement of a kingdome by the peares and nobility.

arithmeticke, [gr] art of numbring

arke, shippe or chest

armorie, [fr] house of armour

arrerages, [fr] debt vnpaid, or things left vndone and duties comming behind.

arrest, stay, or lay hold of

arride, to please well, to content

arriue, [fr] }
arriuall,   } come to land, or approch.

arrogate, to claime, or challenge

arrogant, proude, presumptuous.

artifice, skill, subtiltie: or a cunning peece of worke

artificer, handicrafts-man

artificially, workmanlike, cunningly

articulate, ioynted, set together, or to point out, and distinguish

artichock, [k] herbe

artillery, [fr] engines or instruments for war.

ascend, goe vp, or clime vp

ascent, a going vp

ascribe, giue to, adde to, attribute vnto

askey,
asquint, } looking aside, or awry.

assay, [fr] proofe, or a triall:

assent, agreement, or consent

assertaine, assure: certaine

assentation, flattery: speaking faire

aspect, looking vpon, beholding much, sight

aspectable, worthie, or easie to be seene.

asperat, rough, sharpe, or vnpleasant.

asperation, breathing.

aspire, climbe vp, or come to, or high.

assault, [fr]
assaile, [fr] } to set vpon, or to proue.

assemble, [fr] gather together.

assemblie, companie

assent, consent.

assertion, affirming, auouching of any thing

asseueration, earnest affirming

assiduitie continuance, diligence

assigne, appoint, ordaine

assignation, appointment.

assimulate, to make like, to compare with.

assistance, helpe

assotiation, ioyning together in fellowship.

associate, to accompanie, or follow

assoyle, [fr] excuse, cleare

astipulation, an auouching, or witnessing of a thing, an
   agreement

astrictiue,
astringent, } binding, or ioyning together.

astronomie, [gr]
astrologie, [gr] } knowledge of the starres.

astrolabe, [gr] an instrument to know the motion of the starres.

atheist, [gr]
atheall, } without, God, or beleeuing that there is no God,
      or denying any of his attributes.

atheisme, [gr] the opinion of the atheist.

attach, [fr] sease vpon, rest, or hold

attaint, [fr] conuict of crime

attainder,[fr, a conuiction, or prouing guiltie of a crime or fault.

attempt, [fr] set vpon, or take in hand

attendance, watching, staying for, or wayting vpon.

attentiue, heedie, or marking

attenuate, to make thinner or weaker

attest, to witnesse, or call to witnesse

attrap, ensnare

attribute, giue to, or impute.

auarice, couetousnes, or inordinate desire of money.

auburne [k] colour

audience, hearing, or hearkening, or those that heare.

audacious, bold, rash, or foolish hardie

auditor, hearer, or officer of accounts

audible, easie to be heard.

auer, auouch, call to witnes, proue.

auert, to turne from, or keepe away.

augment, to encrease

auguration, guessing, or coniecturing at things to come:

avowable, [fr] that which may be allowed and affirmed

avouch, [fr] affirme with earnest, defend.

auoke, to call from, or pull back

austere, sharpe, rough, cruell

authenticall, [gr] of authoritie, allowed by authoritie: the originall

autumne, the haruest

axiome, [gr] a certaine principle, or general ground of any Art:

ay, euer, at any time, for euer

azure, [k] of colour.

B

BAile, suretie, witnes.

ballance, a paire of scales, or other thing.

balase, [fr] grauell, wherewith ships are poysed to goe vpright: or weight.

bang, beat

bankerupt, bankerout, waster

banquet, feast.

baptisme, [gr] dipping, or sprinkling.

band, [fr] company of men, or an assembly.

baptist, a baptiser

barbarian, a rude person

barbell, [k] fish

barbarie, [k] of fruite

barbarisme, barbarousnes, rudenes

barke, [fr] small ship

barnacle, [k] bird

barrester, one allowed to giue counsell, or to pleade:

barreter, a contentious person, quarreller, or fighter:

barter, [fr] to bargaine, or change

baud, whore

bauin, a faggot, or kid

bashfull, blush, or shamefast
battrie, [fr] beating or striking
bay, [k] tree.
beadle, office
beagle, [k] hound
beatitude, blessednes, happines
beldam, parent, or maister:
bellona, the goddesse of warre
benediction, praysing or blessing
beneficiall, profitable
beneuolence, good will, or fauour.
benigne, fauourable, curteous, gentle:
benignitie, gentlenes, or kindnes
benisson, [fr] blessing
bequeath, giue:
bereft, depriued, alone, voide, robd.
besiedge, compasse
betrothed, affianced, or promised in marriage:
bewaile, mone, complaine
biere, [fr] a cophin wherein dead men are carried:
bigamie, [gr] twise maried, or hath had two wiues
billiment, iewell, or garment
bipartite, deuided into two parts
bisket, bread:
bishop, ouer-seer, or prelate
blase, report, publish, shew forth
blaspheme, [gr] to speake ill of God:

blattering, vaine babling

blanch, [fr] to make white, or white lime

bleate, cry

blisse, ioy, or happines.

bonnet, [fr] hat, or cap.

bob, beate

bouge, [fr] stirre, remoue from a place.

boate, ship

braule, wrangle.

brachygraphie, [gr] short writing.

bragard, [fr] fine, trim, proude

brandish, [fr] to shake a sword

breuitie, shortnes

brickle,
brittle, } easiely broken, lymber.

brigand, [fr] a theefe, or robber by the high way side.

brigandine, [fr] coate of defence

brigantine, [fr] a small ship

brothell, keeper of a house of baudry,

brooch, iewell.

bruite, [fr] report, noyse.

buggerie, coniunction with one of the same kinde, or of men
    with beasts.

bugle, glasse

buglasse, [k] herbe

bullyon, coyne

burgesse, [fr] a head man of a towne.

C

CAlamitie, trouble, affliction.

calcinate, to make salt:

calefie, make warme, heate, or chafe.

calygraphie, [gr] fayre writing.

calliditie, craftines, or deceit

calumniation, a discrediting by worde, or false accusation.

camphire, kind of herbe.

capacitie, largenes of a place: conceit, or receiet.

capuchon, [fr] a hood

cancell, [fr] to vndoe, deface, crosse out, or teare

canon, [gr] law, or rule

canonise, [gr] make a saint, to examine by rule:

canopie, couer

capitall, deadly, or great, or woorthy of shame, and punishment:

capable, wise, apt to learne, bigge, or fit to receiue.

capitulation, distinguishing by parts

captious, catching, deceitfull, subtile,

captiue, prisoner

captiuate, make subiect, or a prisoner,

cardinall, chiefe, or principall

carminate, to card wooll, or deuide

carnalitie, fleshlines

carnall, fleshly, pleasing the flesh:

carpe, take exception against, or wrangle.

cassere, [fr] dismisse, put away, or out of office.

casualtie, chaunce or hap

castigation, chaistisement, blaming, correction.

catalogue, [gr] beadroole, or rehearesall of words, or names

category, [gr] an accusation

catechiser, that teacheth the principles of Christian religion.

cathedrall, church, cheife in the diocesse

catharre, a flowing of humors from the head.

catholicke, [gr] vniuersall or generall.

cauill, to iest, scoffe, or reason subtilly

caution, warning, putting in minde, or taking heede

celebrate, holy, make famous, to publish, to commend, to keepe
solemlie

celeritie, swiftnes, hast

celestiall, heauenly, diuine passing excellent.

cement, morter, or lime.

censor, a corrector, a iudge, or reformer of manners

censure, correction, or reformation

centre, [gr] middest of any round thing or circle.

centurion, captaine of a hundren men.

ceruse, white leade, or painting that women vse.

cessement, tribute

chanell, sinke:

character, [gr] the fashion of a Letter, a marke, or stampe:

chaunt, [fr] sing

champion, [fr] wilde field, also a challenger,

chambering, lightnes, and wanton behauiour in priuate places

charter, a grant of any thing confirmed by seale.

cheualrie, [fr] knight-hood

cherubin, order of Angels:

chibball, [k] fruite

chirograph, [gr] hand writing

chiromancie, [gr] telling of fortunes, by the lines in the hands:

chirurgion, [gr] a surgion

choller, [gr] a humor causing anger

chough, [k] bird:

christ, [gr] annointed

chronickler, [gr]
chronographer, } historie writer.

chronicall, [gr] returning at certaine times

chronologie, [gr] storie of times past.

cibaries, meates, nourishment

cider, drink made of apples

circuit, about.

circumcise, to cut the priuie skin

circumference, the round and outmost circuit, or compasse

circumligate, binde about

circumscribe, to compasse about with a line, to limit.

circumspect, heedie, quicke of sight, wise, and dooing matters
    aduisedly.

circumlocution, a speaking of that in many words, which may be said in few

circumstance, a qualitie, that accompaneth any thing, as time, place &c

circumstant, things that are about vs,

circumuent, to close in, to deceaue, or intrap craftily.

citron, [k] fruit

ciuilitie, honest in conuersation, or gentle in behauiour.

clamarus, making a great noyse

chassick, chiefe, and approued,

clauicordes, [fr] mirth,

claritude, cleerenes, renowne,

clemencie, gentlenes, curtesie.

client, he that is defended.

climate, a portion of the worlde betwixt north and south

climactericall, [gr] that which ariseth by degrees, as the sixtie third yeere is climactericall of the seauentie.

clister, medicine

coble, amend

coadiutor, a fellow helper.

cockatrice, a kind of beast

cænation, supper, or a place to sup in

cogitation, thought, musing

cognition, knowledge

cohærence, ioyning, & vniting together.

coin, [fr] corner

collect, gather together

colleague, companion,

collaterall, on the other side, ouer against, as two lines drawne
    equally distant one from another, in due place

collation, recitall, a short banquet

collect, gather

collusion, deceit, cousanage

colume, one side of a page of a booke

combine, heale, or couple together,

combination, a ioyning, or coupling together

combure, burne, or consume with fire

combustible, easily burnt

combustion, burning or consuming with fire.

comedie, [k] stage play,

comicall, handled merily like a comedie

commemoration, rehearsing or remembring

commencement, [fr] a beginning or entrance

comet, [gr] a blasing starre

comentarie, exposition of any thing

commerce, fellowship, entercourse of merchandise.

commination, threatning, or menacing,

commiseration, pittie

commodious, profitable, pleasant, fit,

commotion, rebellion, trouble, or disquietnesse.

communicate, make partaker, or giue part vnto

communaltie, [fr] common people, or common-wealth

communion,
communitie, } fellowship.

compact, ioyned together, or an agreement.

compassion, pitty, fellow-feeling

compell, to force, or constraine

compendious, short, profitable

compensation, a recompence:

compeare, like

competent, conuenient, sufficient, apt:

competitor, hee that sueth for the same thing, or office, that another doth:

compile, gather together

complement, perfecting of any thing

complet, fulfilled, finished

Complexion, nature, constitution of the body.

complices, [fr] fellowes in wicked matters

compose, make, or ioyne together

composition, agreement, a making, or mingling together.

comprehend,
comprise, } to containe.

comprimise, agreement, made by parties chosen on either side

comprimit, iudge

compte, fine, decked: trimmed

compulsion, force, constraint

computation, an account or reckoning

compunction, pricking

concauitie, hollownes

conceale, to keepe close

conception, conceiuing in the wombe.

concinnate, made fit, finely apparelled

concise, briefe or short

concoct, to digest meate

concord,
concordance, } agreement.

concrete, ioyned, or congealed together

concruciate, to torment, or vex together

concubine, harlot, or light huswife.

conculcate, to treade vnderfoote

concupiscence, desire

concurre, agree together, runne together, or meete.

concurse, running together of many to a place.

condigne, worthie

condiscende, agree vnto, or consent

condole, to be greeued, or sorrowfull with another.

conduct, guiding, or hiring

confabulate, to talke together

confection, compounding, making or mingling.

confederate, agreeing peaceably together by couenants made

conferre, talke together

conference, communication, talking together.

confidence, trust, hope

confine, to border vpon, to compasse in

confirme, establish

confiscation, [fr] forfeiture or losse of goods

conflict, battaile, strife, fight

conforme, to make like vnto, consent

confound, ouerthrow, destroy, mingle together, or disorder.

confront, [fr] opposse, compare one to another.

congeale, to harden, or ware hard, or freeze together.

congestion, a heaping vp

conglutinate, to ioyne together

congratulate, to reioyce with another for some good fortune.

congregate, gather together

congruence,
congruitie, } agreablenes, or likenes.

coniunction, ioyning together

coniure, to conspire together, to sweare by.

connexion, ioyning together

conuiuence, sufferance, or winking at

conquest, a complayning, or victorie

consanguinitie, kinred by blood, or birth

consecrate, make holie, to dedicate, or giue vnto.

consectarie, one that followeth any opinion.

consent, agreement

consequence,
consequent, } following by order.

conserue, keepe, saue, or maintaine

consideratly, wisely, and with aduise, consist, stand

consistorie, [fr] place of ciuill iudgement

consociate, companie with, or ioyne a companion vnto.

consolation, comfort

consonant, agreeable, likelie

consort, a companion, or company

conspicuous, easie to be seene, excellent

conspire, agree together, for to doe euill.

constellation, a company of starrs

constitutions, lawes, or decrees

construe, expound

consul, a chiefe gouernor among the Romanes.

consult, take counsaile

consumate, accomplish, fulfill, or finish.

contagious, that which corrupteth, or infecteth.

contaminate, defiled, or corrupted

contaminouse, infectious, defiled

contemplation, meditation, or musing

contend, wrangle

contestate, to call to witnes

context, the agreeing of the matter going before, with that which followeth.

continent, modest, abstaining, chast: also the firme land where no ile or sea is.

contingent, happening by chaunce

contract, make short, also a bargaine, or couenant.

contradiction, gaine saying

contribute, bestowe vpon, or giue vnto

contribution, a bestowing of any thing

contributorie, giuing a part to any thing

contrite, broken, sorrowfull

contrition, sorrow, sadnes

contriue, make

contumacie, stubbornnes, contempt

contumelie, slaunder, reproch

contusion, bruised, or beaten

conuent, bring before a iudge

conuenient, fit, well beseeming

conuenticle, a little assemblie

conuerse, companie with

conuert, turne, change

conuict, proued guiltie, ouercome

conuince, to ouercome, confute, or proue manifestly.

conuocation, an assembling, or calling together.

conuoy, [fr] a waiting vppon: or keeping company in the way.

connulsion, a pulling, or shrinking vp

copartner, fellow partaker, or companion

cophin, [gr] basket, or chest for a dead body to be put in.

copious, plentifull, abounding

copulation, ioyning, or coupling together

cordwainer, shoemaker, or trade

cordiall, comforting the hart.

coriuals, [fr] competitors

carnositie, full of flesh, grosse

corporall, bodily

corporate, hauing a bodie:

corps, [fr] deade bodie

corpulent, grosse of body, fat, or great

correspondent, answerable

correllatiues, when 2. things are so linked together, that the one cannot be without the otherr.

corrigible, easily corrected

corroborate, confirme, or strengthen, or make strong.

corroded, gnawd about

corrosiue, fretting

cosmographie, [gr] description of the world.

costiue, bound in the bodie

couch, [fr] bed, lie downe:

couert, [fr] hidden place, secrete

counterchange, [fr] to change againe:

countermaund, [fr] commaund contrarie

countermine, [fr] vndermine one against another.

countermure, [fr] to builde, one wall against another.

crassitude, fatnesse or thicknesse

counterpoise, [fr] make leuell, or to weigh, as heuie as another
  thing.

cowslip, [k] hearb

counteruaile, [fr] of equall valew

credence, beliefe

curbe, [fr] restraine, keepe in:

credible, which may be beleeued

couerture, [fr] couering

creditor, he which lendeth, or trusteth another:

credulous, readie to belieue, true

credulitie, rashnes in belieuing

creuas, [fr] rift.

crible, [fr] sifted

criminous,
criminall, } faultie, that wherein is some fault.

crisped, curled, or frisled.

criticall, [gr] which giueth iudgement of sicknes. &c.

crocodile, [k] beast

crucifie, fasten to a crosse

crude, raw, not ripe, not digested:

crupt, [gr] hidden, or secret

crystaline, [gr] cleere like glasse, or christall.

cubite, a foote and a halfe

culpable, blame-worthy, guiltie,

culture, husbandry, tilling.

curiositie, picked diligence, greater carefulnes, then is seemely or necessarie,

cursorilie, swiftly, or briefely.

curuefie, bowed, or made crooked.

custodie, keeping, or looking to

cymball, an instrument of musicke, so called.

cynicall, [gr] doggish, froward.

cypher, [gr] a circle in numbering, of no value of it selfe, but serueth to make vp the number, and to make other figures of more value.

D

DAmnable, not to be allowed.

deacon, [gr] prouider for the poore

demonaicke, [gr] possessed with a deuill.

deambulation, a walking abroade

debate, [fr] strife, contention

debar, let:

debilitie, weakenes, faintnes.

debonnayre, [fr] gentle, curteous, affable,

decalogue, [gr] the ten commaundements:

decacordon, [gr] an instrument with tenne strings

decent, comlie, or beseeming

decease, a departing, or giuing place too.

decide, to determine, or make an end of.

decipher, describe, or open the meaning, or to count.

decision, cutting away.

declamation, an oration of a matter feyned.

decline, fall away, or swarue from,

decoction, liquor, wherein things are sod for phisicke.

decorum, comlines

decrepite, very old

dedicate, to giue for euer.

deduct, take or drawe out, abate, or diminish.
deface, [fr] blot out, staine, bring out of fashion
defame, to slaunder, or speake ill of
defect, want, fayling
defie, [fr] distrust.
define, to shew clearely what a thing is.
deflower, dishonest, rauish, or disgrace
deformed, ill shapen, ill fauored
defraude, [fr] deceiue, beguile
defraye, [fr] lay out, pay, discharge
degenerate, be vnlike his auncestours: to grow out of kind.
dehort, mone or perswade from, to aduise to the contrarie.
deitie, Godhead
deifie, make like God
delectation, delight, or pleasure
delegate, an imbassadour, or one appointed in anothers place
deliberate, to take good counsell
delineate, to drawe the proportion of any thing.
delicate, daintie, giuen to pleasure
delude, deceiue, or laugh to scorne.
deluge, [fr] great floode, or ouer flowing of waters.
delusion, mockerie, a deceitfull thing
demaund, request, aske
demerite, deseruing, worthines
democracie, [gr] a common-wealth gouerned by the people.
demonstrate, shew plainely, or openly, to point out or manifest.
demenour, behauiour

demurre, [fr] to stay, to linger, or vse delaies

denison, free borne

denounce, declare, or giue warning of, or proclaime

denomination, a naming

depend,
dependance, } hang vpon.

deplore, to lament or bewaile

deplume, to pull of the feathers

deportation, carrying away

depopulate, spoile, or wast

depose, put away, depriue, or put downe.

dapraue, marre or corrupt, or make worse.

deprecation, supplication, or requiring of pardon

depresse, to keepe downe

depriue, see depose

depute, account, or esteeme

deride, mock, or laugh to scorne.

derision, mocking

deriue, fetch from

deriuation, taking away from some other matter.

derogate, to take away, or to diminish

desastrous, [fr] vnluckie, vnfortunate

descend, goe downe.

describe, to write foorth, to copie out, or to declare

deseigne, [fr]
deseignment, [fr], } an appoynting how any thing shall be done.

desert, wildernesse.

desertion, a leauing, or forsaking

designe, to marke out, or appoint for any purpose:

desist, leaue off, or stay

desolate, left alone, or forsaken

desperate, without hope, or past hope,

detect, bewray, disclose, accuse

destinated, appointed,

destitute, forsaken

detest, hate greatly, or abhorre

deteined, withholden, or kept back,

determine, resolue, conclude

detract, take from, or backbite

detriment, losse or hurt

detrude, thrust out, or from

deuote, to giue vnto, or appoint vnto

deuotion, holinesse.

deuoyre, [fr] dutie

dexteritie, aptnes, nimblenes

diabolicall, [gr] deuillish.

diademe, [gr] a Kings crowne:

diapason, [gr] a concorde in musick of all parts

diet, manner of foode

dialect, the manner of speech in any language, diuers from
     others.

dialogue, [gr] conference, or talking together.

diameter, [gr] a line, crossing the midst of any circle or figure

didacticall, [gr] full of doctrine or instruction.

diffamation, a slaundering, or speaking ill of:

different, vnlikely, disagreeing,

difficill,
difficult, } hard, vneasie, dangerous

diffident, mistrustfull

diffude, poure out

digest, bring into order, to deuide, & distribute things into their right place.

dignitie, worthinesse

digresse, turne from, goe away

digression, departing from the matter in hand

dilacerate, to rent in sunder:

dilate, enlarge, spread abroade, or to discourse vpon largely

dilemma, [gr] a forked kinde of argument, which on either side entrappeth.

dimension, measuring

diminution, lessening

diocesse, [gr] iurisdiction

diocesan, that hath iurisdiction

direct, guide, or rule: right, straight, also to order.

disable, make vnable, or finde fault with.

disabilitie, vnablenes

disaduantageous, [fr] hindering much

disanull, make voyde, or bring to nothing.

disburse, [fr] lay out money

discent, comming downe from another

discerne, know, put one from another, or put difference

discide, cut off, or in peeces

discipline, instruction, or training vp.

disciple, scholler,

discipher, to lay open, or make plaine

disclose, discouer, vtter, or manifest.

discomfiting, [fr] putting to flight

discord, disagreement, variance

discretion, wise choise of one from another

discusse, examine, debate, or search narrowly into:

disfigure, bring out of shape,

disfranchis, [fr] take away freedome:

disioyne, vnioyne, or seperate

disiunction, a deuiding, or seperating,

disfranchised, [fr] depriued of libertie.

disgrade, to discharge of his orders, or degrees.

disguised, [fr] counterfeited, seeming that it is not:

dislocation, setting out of right place,

disloyall, [fr] one whom it is not good to trust, vntrustie,
   trayterous.

dismember, to pull and part one peece from another.

dismisse, let passe, or send away

disparagement, hurt, hinderance, or disgrace:

dispence, to giue licence vnto

disperse, scatter, or spread abroade.

dispeople, to vnpeople a place

displant, to pull vp by the rootes, trees planted.

display, spread abroade

dispose, to set in order, to appoint.

disposition, naturall inclination, or setting in order.

dispoyle, take away by violence, or rob

disputable, questionable, or doubtfull, that may be reasoned of:

dissent, disagree, to be of a contrarie opinion.

dissimilitude, vnlikenes

dissimulation, dissembling

dissipation, scattering abroade

dissolue, vnloose, or melte

dissoluble, easie to vnloose

dissolute, carelesse, rechlesse

dissolution, breaking, vnloosing.

dissonant, disagreeing

distance, space betweene

distended, stretched out, or out of ioynt.

distinguish, put difference, deuide, or point out from others.

distillation,
distilling, } dropping downe by little and little.

distinct, differing, or deuided

distinction, a difference, or seperation

distracted, drawne into diuerse parts

distribute, deuide in sunder, or to giue in sundrie parts.

distribution, diuision, or laying out by parts.

disturbe, disquiet, let, or interrupt

disswade, to perswade to the contrarie

dittie, the matter of a song.

diuert, turne from, to another

diuine, Heauenly godly, also to gesse, coniecture, or prophesie.
diuinitie, heauenly, doctrine, also godhead.
diuision, parting, or seperating
diurnall, a daily mouing
divulgate, publish, or make common
docilitie, easie to be taught
doctrine, learning, or instruction
dolor, griefe, sorrow, or paine
dolorous, grieuous, or sorrowfull
domage, [fr] losse, harme, or hinderance
domesticall, at home, belonging to houshold: priuate
dominere, rule, beare sway
domicilles, houses
dominion,
domination, } rule, lordship or maistership.
donatiue, a gift, in money or other things
dulcimur,
dulcimar, [k] } instrument.
duarchy, the equall raigne of two princes together.
driblets, small debts
dulcifie, sweeten
dulcor, sweetnesse
durable, long lasting, or of long continuance.

E

Ebullient, seething

ebulliated, boyled

[e]clipse, [gr] failing of the light of the sunne or moone

eccho, a sound, resounding back againe

ecclesiasticall, [gr] belonging to the church

eden, pleasure, or delight

edict, a commaundement from authoritie, a proclamation.

edifice, building

edifie, instruct, or builde vp in knowledge.

edition, putting foorth, setting abroade

education, bringing vp

effect, a thing done, or to bring to passe

effectuall, forcible

effeminate, womannish, delicate, wanton.

efficacie, force, or strength

efficient, working, or accomplishing

effusion, powring, or running foorth

eglogue, [gr] a talking together

egresse, foorthgoing, or passage out

eiection, a casting foorth

elaborate, done curiously, and dilligently.

election, choise

elect, chosen, or picked out

elegancie, finesse of speech

element, the first principle or beginning of anything.

elench, [gr] a subtill argument

eleuate, lift vp, or heaue vp

elocution, good vtterance of speech.

emerods, [k] of disease

embark, [fr] } to ship a thing, or load a ship.
imbark,

emblem, [gr] a picture shadowing out some thing to be learned.

eminent, appearing, higher, or further out, excelling.

emmot, pismire

emphasis, [gr] a forcible expressing

empire, [fr] gouernement: or kingdome

emulation, enuie, or imitate

enarration, declaration, expounding

enigmaticall, [gr] full of hard questions, obscure.

enchaunt, [fr] bewitch

encounter, set against, or to meete

encrochment, [fr] when the Lord hath gotten seisen of more rent, or seruices of his tenant then of right is due.

endosse, [fr] cut on the back, or write on the back.

enduce, moue

enimitie, } displeasure, or hatred.
enmitie,

enflame, burne, or set on fire.

enfranchise[fr], make free

engrate, [fr] presse vpon

enhaunce, [fr] to lift vp, or make greater:

enlarge, [fr] make bigger, set at libertie

enoble, [fr] make noble, or famous

enormious, out of square, vnorderly

ensigne, [fr] flagge for war

enterlace, [fr] to put betweene, intermingle:

enterprise, [fr] beginne, take in hand

enterre, [fr] lay in the earth

entrals, [fr] inward parts, as hart, liuer, &c.

enuiron, [gr] to enclose, or compasse about.

epha, kind of measure

epicure, giuen to pleasure.

epigram, [gr] a sentence, written vpon any for praise, or dispraise

epilogue, [gr] conclusion

epilepsis, [gr] the falling sicknes

episcopall, [gr] bishoplike.

epiphanie, [gr] appearing

epitaph, [gr] the writing on a tombe or graue.

epithite, [gr] a name or title giuen to any thing.

epitome, [gr] the briefe copie of a booke, &c.

epitomise, [gr] to make an epitome, or to bring a booke into a lesser volume.

equalize, match, or make equall

equinoctium, when the dayes and nights are equall.

equipage, [fr] furniture

equitie, right, lawfulnes

erect, set vp, or lift vp

equiualent, of equall valew.

ermite, [gr] one dwelling in the wildernes.

erronious, full of errour, and wandring out of the right way.

essay, [fr] tryall what one can say, or doe in any matter.

escheat, [fr] forfaite

eschew, [fr] shunning, auoyde, escape

espoused, [fr] promised in marriage

essence, substance, or being of any thing

essoine, [fr] excused for any cause

establish, [fr] confirme, make strong

estimate, esteeme, value, or prise, thinke or iudge.

eternall, euerlasting, without end

ethnick, [gr] an heathen, or gentile

etymologie, [gr] true expounding

euacuated, made voyde, cleane taken away: or emptied.

euangell, [gr] the gospell: or glad tidings

euangelist, [gr] bringer of glad tidings

euaporate, to breath out

euent, chaunce, or that which followeth any thing.

euict, ouercome by law

eucharist, [gr] a thanksgiuing, the Lords supper.

eunuch, [gr] gelded, wanting stones

euert, turne vpside downe

euident, easie to be seene, plaine

euocation, calling forth

exact, perfectly done, or to require with extremitie.

exaggerate, heape vpon, amplifie to make a thing more then it is

exaltation, lifting vp

exasperate, whet on, to vex, or make more angrie

excauate, make hollow

excæcate, to make blind

excessiue, too much, more then enough

excheaquer, [fr] office of receits

exclaime, bray, or crie out

exclude, thrust, or shut out, or keepe out

excogitate, to muse, or deuise exactly.

excommunicate, to thrust out of company, or fellowship

excrement, dung, offal, refuse, or dregs.

excruciat, to vex, or torment

excursion, a skirmidsh in warres, of some few running from their companie

execrable, cursed

execute, performe, or exercise some charge

exempt, free, priuiledged.

exemplifie, enlarge, or declare by examples

exhalation, a breath, or fume rising vpward

exhaust, drawne out, or emptied

exhibite, put vp or bestow: to offer, or set abroade for all men to see

exiccate, to drie vp

exile, banish, driue out

exorable, easie, to be intreated

exorbitant, out of order, measure or place.

exorcist, [gr] coniurer

exorde, [fr] beginne

exordium, a beginning, or entrance

expect, looke for

expedient, fit, meete or beseeming

expedition, hast, speede

expell, put out, or thrust out

expend, consider, or muse vpon

expence, cost, or money layd out

experiment, a proofe, or triall

expert, skilfull

expiation, pacifying with satisfaction, purging by sacrifice

expire, to die, or giue vp the ghost to decay.

explane, to make manifest, or delcare

explicate, declare plainely

exploit, [fr] enterprise, act, deede

expose, to offer, or lay open, to hazard,

expostulate, to reason, or chide with, to complaine:

expresly, fitly, manifestly

exprobration, vpbreyding, casting in ones teeth.

expugnable, to be wonne, or ouercome.

expulse, driue out, or thrust out

exquisite, perfect, fine, singuler, curious.

extant, appearing, abroad, shewing it selfe.

extasie, a traunce, or sowning.

extemporall,
extempore, } suddaine, without premeditation, or studie.
extemporarie,
extende, spread foorth, prolong, or make longer, to inlarge.
extenuate, lessen, minish, or make lesse.
externall, outward, strange
extinguish, put out, or quench
extinct, put out
extirpate, to pull vp by the rootes
extoll, aduaunce, or praise highly, to lift vp
extort, to wring out, to wrest from by violence.
extract, drawne out
extrauagant, wandring out of order.
exulcerate, to make sore, to corrupt.

F

Fabricate, make, fashion.

fabulous, fained, counterfeited, much talked of

fact, deede

facilitie, easines

faction, deuision of people into sundry parts and opinions

factious, that maketh deuision, contentious.

factor, one that doth busines for another

facultie, licence, power, aptnes

fallacie, deceit, falshood

falsifie, to forge, or counterfait

fame, report, common talke, credite

fantacie, imagination

fantastique, [fr] conceited, full of deuises

farce, [fr] to fill, or stuffe

falcinate, to bewitch, or disfigure by inchauntment.

fastidiousnes, lothsomnesse, or disdainfullnesse

faschious, [fr] grieuous, or inducing to anger.

fatall, mortall, appointed by God to come to passe.

fealtie, [fr] faithfulnes

fecunditie, fruitfulnesse

felicitie, happinesse

female, [fr] ⎫
feminine, ⎬ the she in mankind, or other creatures.

fermentated, leauened

feruide, hote, scalding, burning

festination, hast, speede

festiuitie, mirth, pleasantnes

festiuall, merrie, pertaining to holy daies

feruent, hote, chafed, verie angrie

fertile, fruitfull, yeelding much fruit

feuer, ague

fiction, a lie, or tale fained

fidelitie, faithfulnes, trustines

figurate, to shadowe, or represent, or to counterfaite

figuratiue, by figures

finall, pertaining to the end

finite, hauing an end, and certaine limits.

firme, sure, stedfast, strong, constant

fixed, fastned, sure, fast

flagon, [fr] great wine cup, or bottell

flagrant, burning, hot

flexible, easilie bent, pliant, or mutable

flote, [fr] swime aloft

fluxible, thin, and running easily downe like water.

floscles, [fr] flowers

fluxe, disease of scouring

feeble, [fr] weake, lacking strength

fomentation, an asswaging, or comforting by warmth.

foraine, strange, of another country

formall, following the common fashion

foraminated, holed, or bored

formidable, fearefull, to be feared

fornication, vncleannes betweene single persones.

fortification, strengthning

fortitude, valiantnes, or couragiousnes, strength

fortunate, happie, hauing good successe

fragilitie, brittlenes, or weakenes

fragments, reliques, broken meates, peeces broken of.

fragrant, sweetly smelling

franck, [fr] liberall, bountiful

fraternitie, brotherhood

franchise, [fr] libertie, freedome

fraudulent, deceitfull, craftie, or ful of guile.

frequent, often, done many times: ordinarie, much haunted, or goe too.

frigifie, coole, make cold

friuolous, vaine, trifeling, of no estimation.

frontlet, [k] attire for the fore-head

fructifie, to make fruitfull, or bring foorth much fruit.

frugall, thriftie, temperate in expences

fruition, inioying, possession

frustrate, make voyde, deceiue

fugitiue, runnagate, or starting away

fulgent, glistering, or shining

fuluide, yellowe

fume, to yeeld smoke

function, calling, or charge, or trade, and place wherein a man
liueth.

funerall, buriall, mourning: pertaining to a buriall, or mourning.

furbush, to dresse or scoure, or make cleane

furniture, [fr] all things necessary to vse

furious, raging, or mad

future, that which shall be heereafter

G

garboile, [fr] hurlie burly

gardian, a keeper, or defendor

gargarise, to wash the mouth, and throate within, by stirring
some liquor vp and downe in the mouth,

garnar,
granar, } corne, or corne chamber.

garnish, [fr] trime, decke vp, make fine.

gem, a precious stone

gaie, [fr] fine, trim

gentilitie,
generositie, } gentrie, nobilitie, gentlemanship.

genesis, [gr] beginning

gentile, a heathen

generation, ofspring

genealogie, [gr] generation, or a describing of the stock or
pedegree.

genitalles, priuities

genuine, peculiar, or naturall

genius, the angell that waits on man, be it a good or euill angell

genitor, father

geographie, [gr] the describing of the earth.

geometrie, [gr] art of measuring the earth.

geomancie, [gr] sorcerie by circkles, and pricks in the earth

germane, come of the same stock

gests, things done, or noble acts of princes

gibbocitie, crookednes

gire, grin, or laugh

giues, fetters

glee, mirth, gladnes

gospell, glad tidings

globe, any thing, very round.

glorifie, to giue honour, praise, and commendation to any body.

glosse, a tongue, or exposition of a darke speech.

gloze, dissemble

gourmandise, [fr] deuouring, gluttony

glutinate, to glue, or ioyne together

gnible, bite

gnomen, [gr] the stile, or cock of a diall

gradation, steps, by little and little.

graduate, that hath taken a degree

gratifie, to pleasure, or doo a good turne in way of thankfulnes

gratis, freely, without desert

gratitude, thankfulnes

gratulate, to be glad for anothers sake,

graue, waightie, sober, sage, discreete

grease, fat

guerdon, [fr] a reward:

guidance, [fr] gouerning, or direction

guise, [fr] fashion, shape, custome,
gulfe, deepe poole, or pit
gustation, taste

H

HAbilitie,
abilitie, } ablenes, or of sufficiencie.

habitable, able to dwell in

habitacle,
habitation, } a dwelling place:

habite, apparell, fashion, custome

habitude, disposition, plight, respect

hale, [fr] pull, draw, lift vp

halaluiah, praise the Lord

hallucinate, to deceiue, or blind

harmonie, [gr] agreement of diuers sounds in musicke.

hautie, [fr] loftie, proude

hazard, [fr] venture, chaunce:

herault, [fr] kings messenger

heathen, see Gentile

hebrew, from Hebers stock

hecticke, [gr] inflaming the hart, and soundest parts of the bodie

hemisphere, [gr] halfe of the compasse of heauen, that we see.

helmet, head peece,

hereditarie, comming by inheritance, or succession:

heritage, inheritance, possession

herbinger, sent before to prepare

hereticall, [gr]
hereticke, [gr] } one that maintaineth heresies.

hermite, see ermite

heroicall, [gr] beseeming a noble man, or magnificent:

hideous, [fr] fearefull, terrible

hierarchie, [gr] the gouernment of priests, or holy gouernance:

hymne, [gr] kinde of song to the prayse of GOD.

hipocrite, [gr] such a one as in his outward apparrell, countenaunce, & behauiour, pretendeth to be another man, then he is indeede, or a deceiuer.

historicall, [gr] pertaining to historie

homage, [fr] worship, or seruice.

homicide, [fr] a man killer, or the killing of a man:

hononimie, [gr] when diuers things are signified by one word

horror, fearefull sorrow, feare, terror.

horizon, [gr] a circle, deuiding the halfe of the firmament, from the other halfe which we see not.

hosanna, saue now:

hospitality, good entertainement for friends and strangers.

hostage, [fr] pledge

hostilitie, hatred, or enmitie, or open wars.

huckster, marchant, or trade

humane, belonging to man, gentle, curteous, bounteous.

humide, wet,

humiditie, moysture

hush,
husht, } peace, or be still.

hyperbolicall, [gr] beyond all credite, or likelihoode of truth.

I

Idiome, [gr] a proper forme or speech:

idiot, [gr] vnlearned, a foole

Iehoua, Lord almighty

ientation, breakefast

ieoperdie, danger

Iesus, Sauiour.

ignoble, of low and base birth

ignominie, reproch, discredite, slaunder:

illegitemate, vnlawfully begotten, and borne.

illiquinated, vnmelted

illiterate, vnlearned, without knowledge.

illustrate, to make plaine, to declare

illuminate, to inlighten, or make plaine

illusion, mockerie, iesting, or scoffing

imbecilitie, weakenes, feeblenes

imbarge, ⎫
imbarke, ⎬ see embarke

imitation, following, dooing the like:

immaculate, vnspotted, vndefiled

immanitie, beastlie, crueltie, or hugenesse and greatnes

immature, vnripe, or out of season:

immediate, next to, not hauing any other betwixt
imminent, at hand, ready to come vpon
immoderate, without measure, exceeding great, or excessiue
immortall, euerlasting, that dieth not
immunitie, freedome from any thing, or libertie:
immure, to shut vp, or inclose within wals
immutable, constant, still the same, vnchangable:
impart, [fr] to make partaker of, to tell to
impacience, lacke of sufferance
impaire, [fr] diminish, lessen
impeach, [fr] accuse, hurt, or hinder
impediment, let, or hinderance
impenetrable, that cannot be pierced, or entred into:
impenitent, vnrepentant:
imperated, commaunded, or ruled ouer
imperious, desiring to rule, full of commaunding, stately
imperfection, vnperfectnes
imperiall, belonging to the crowne
impertinent, not pertaining to the matter.
impetrate, obtaine by request
impetuous, violent
impietie, vngodlines, crueltie
implacable, that cannot be pleased or pacified.
implement, stuffe:
imply, to signifie, or make manifest
imploy, bestow, spend
implore, to desire with teares,

implume, to pull off the feathers

impose, lay vpon, or put on

importance, of value, force, or worth:

impost, [fr] tribute

imposture, falshood, deceit,

impotent, weake, feeble,

importune, to be earnest with

importunate, requiring earnestly, without beeing satis-fied, till the request be obteyned.

imprecation, cursing, or wishing euill vnto.

impregnable, [fr] vnuanquished, not able to be ouercome, strong.

impression, printing, marking, or stamping:

improper, vnfit, vnseemely, common

impropriation, a thing accounted poper, which is not indeede

improbable, that cannot be prooued.

improuident, carelesse, not foreseeing, or taking heede before hand.

imprudent, ignorant, rash, carelesse:

impudent, shamelesse,

impugne, resist:

impunitie, lack, or omission of punishment

impuritie, filthines, vncleannesse, dishonestie.

impute, reckon, or assigne, blame, or to lay to ones charge

inabilitie, want of power or abilitie.

inamored, in loue with.

inaugurate, to aske counsell of soothsayers.

incarnate, taking flesh vpon him, or to bring flesh vpon.

incense, kind of offering made by fire

incend, kindle, burne, vexe, or chafe, to incense, to stirre vp, or to set on fire, or to anger.

incessantlie, earnestlie, without ceasing

incest, vnlawfull copulation of man and woman within the degrees of kinred, or alliance, forbidden by gods law, whether it be in marriage or otherwise.

inchaunt, bewitch, or charme

incident, happening, or chauncing

incision, cutting, in searching of a wound

incitate, to moue, or prouoke

incline, leane vnto, or towards

include, to shut in, or containe within

incommodious, hurtfull, vnfit

incommunicable, that cannot bee imparted to any other, or proper to one person, and none other.

incomperable, that hath not his like

incompatible, insufferable

incomprehensible, that cannot be conceiued, or vnderstood

incongruencie, want of agreement

inconsiderate, rash, not taking counsaile

incontinent, liuing loosely, or vnchastly

incontinently, presently, disorderly, or without moderation.

incredible, marueilous, such as cannot be beleeued.

incorporate, to graft one thing into the bodie of another, to make one bodie or substance of two or moe, to mixe or put together.

incorruptible, vncorruptible, vnperishable, or not subiect to
    corruption

incredulous, hardly brought to beleeue

inculcate, to vrge, or repeate one thing often:

inculpable, without fault, blamelesse,

incurable, past cure, a wound that cannot be healed:

incur, runne into

indecent, not comly, or beseeming,

indeere, make bound to one,

indefinite, without rule, or order, not determined:

indemnitie, without losse

indignitie, vnworthinesse, vnseemly vsage, infamie, or disgrace

indignation, anger, chafing,

indissoluble, that cannot be vnloosed or vndoone:

indite, [fr] to signifie, or giue in ones name.

induce, to moue vnto, or allure, or draw:

indulgence, sufferance, too gentle intreating.

induction, bringing in

indurate, harden.

industrie, diligence or labour

ineffable, vnspeakable, that cannot be vttered

inequalitie, vnlikenes

inestimable, that cannot be valued, or accounted of as it
    deserueth.

ineuitable, that cannot be auoyded.

inexorable, that cannot, or will not be intreated to graunt

infallible, vndeceiueable, vnguilefull, trustie.

infamous, ill reported of, or defamed
infatuate, to make foolish.
infection, corrupting
infernall, belonging to hell,
inferre, bring in, to alleage, or signifie
infidelitie, vnfaithfulnes:
infinite, without number, or end
infirmitie, weakenes:
inflamation, inflaming, or setting on fire
inflexible, that cannot be bended, vnruly.
inflict, to lay vpon
influence, a flowing in.
informe, giue notice to teach, to beginne to instruct.
infringe, to breake, to make weake, or feeble.
infuse, to poure in, or steepe in,
ingage, [fr] lay to pledge, binde himselfe
ingratitude, vnkindness, or vnthankfulnes
ingenious, wittie, quicke witted
ingine,
engine, } an instrument to doo any thing with.
ingraue, [fr] carue
ingresse,
ingredience, } enterance in.
ingurgitate, to deuoure vp greedily
inhabite, dwell in
inhabitable, that cannot be dwelt in
inherent, cleauing fast vnto,

inhibit, forbid.

inhibition, forbidding.

inhumane, cruell, vncurteous.

iniunction, commaunding, rule or order.

initiate, to begin, instruct, or enter into

iniurious, wrongfull, or hurtfull,

innauigable, that cannot be sailed vpon

innouate, make newe, young, begin.

innouation, making new, an alteration.

inoculated, grafted, or vnholed.

inordinate, out of order, disordered,

inquinate, to defile, or disgrace

inquisitiue, desirous, and diligent to finde out by asking of
   questions.

inquisition, searching, or inquiring.

insatiable, that cannot bee filled or contented.

incend, clime vp, or mount vp

inscription, a title, or note written vppon any place.

inscrutable, that cannot be searched into, or throughly knowne.

insensible, that cannot be felt or perceiued.

inseperable, that cannot be deuided.

insert, to put in, or graft in.

insinuate, creepe into ones fauour craftilie, also to signifie.

insist, to stay vpon:

insociable, that will not keepe company.

insolent, proude, disdainefull,

insperge, sprinkle, or cast vpon

inspire, breath or blow into

instable, inconstant, not steddie.

install, [fr] admit to a place of office, or honour.

instant, earnest, importunate,

instauration, repairing, renewing.

instigation, prouoking, or mouing forward.

instill, to put in, or drop in.

instinct, inward motion, or stirring.

institute, appoint, ordaine, begin, or go in hand with.

insulte, to triumphe, or vaunt ouer.

insupportable, not able to be borne

integritie, purenes, innocencie

intelligence, knowledge from others

intemperate, without measure or meane, vnmodest in behauiour

intende, to purpose, or think

intentiue, earnestly bent, and musing

intercession, going betweene, or making intreatie for another,

intercept, preuent, or take before

interchange, exchang

intercourse, mutuall accesse, or passage one to another

interdict, to forbid straitly

interest, [fr] loane, right, also a part in any thing

interlace, mixe

interline, draw a line betwixt, or to blot out with a penne, and to
     write betwixt

interlocution, interrupting of anothers speech

intermedle, deale with

intermingle, mixe, or mingle with, or amongst

intermission, forestowing, a pawsing, or breaking of

interpellate, disturbed, hindered

interpreter, expounder

interprete, open, make plaine, to shewe the sence and meaning of a thing

interre, to burie

interrogation, a question, or asking

interrupt, breake of, or let

intire, [fr] whole, sound, vncorrupt

intestate, that dieth without making a will

intimate, to declare or signifie

intised, drawne, allured

intituled, [fr] called, noted, written on the beginning

intractable, vnrulie, troublesome

intricate, inwrapped, doubtfull, hard to be knowne.

introduction, entrance, or leading in

intrude, to thrust ones selfe into the company of others, or enter in violently

inuade, to set vpon, to lay hold on

inueigle, intice, or deceiue by subtiltie, to intrape.

inueighe, to raile vppon bitterly

inuentory, [fr] table of goods

inuention, deuise, or imagination

inueloped, [fr] wrapped in, intangled

inuersion, turning vpside downe, turning contrariwise.

inuest, [fr] to adorne, or decke, or grace.

inueterate, of long continuance, growne in custome:

inuincible, not to be wonne

inuisible, that cannot be seene or perceiued:

inuiolable, that cannot be broken

inuite, bid, request

invndation, an ouerflowing by water,

invocation, a calling vpon any thing with trust in the same

irchin, a hedgehog.

ironie, [gr] a mocking speech

irreligious, vngodly, wanting religion

irreprehensible, without reproofe

irreuocable, not to be recalled, or not to bee withdrawne

irritate, to make angry

irruption, breaking in

issue, [fr] euent, or successe, or end:

iterate, to repeat, or do a thing often, or againe:

iubilee, yeere of ioy, which happened to the Iewes euery fiftie
     yeere.

iudaisme, worshipping one God without Christ.

iudiciall, belonging to iudgement

iurisdiction, authoritie, to make, or execute lawes in any place.

iustifie, approoue, or make to be accounted good and iust

iustified made or accounted for righteous, cleane from sinne.

L

laborinth, a place so full of windings and turnings, that a man cannot finde the way out of it:

laborious, painfull, full of labour

language, [fr] a tongue, or speech:

languishing, pining, consuming, wearing away with griefe or sicknes

lapidarie, one skilfull in pretious stones or iewells

largesse, [fr] or largis: liberalitie

lasciuious, wanton, lecherous

lassitude, wearines

latitude, breadth, largnes

lauacre, a bath or font

lauish, to spend extraordinarily

laud, praise, or commendation

laudable, worthie of praise

laxatiue, loose, purging

league, [fr] agreement, or couenant of peace.

leake, runne out.

lecherie, vnchastnesse, luxurie, and vnlawfull lust

leete, [fr] court

legacie, [fr] a gift by will, or an ambassage

legate, ambassadour

legeiredemaine, [fr] lighthandednes, craftie slights, and conueiance

legion, host, or band of souldiers

legitimate, lawfull, according to lawe, and good order

lenitie, gentlenes, mildnes

lethall, mortall, deadly

lethargie, [gr] [k] a drowsie and forgetfull disease.

leuell, right, straight

leuitie, lightnes, inconstancie

libertine, loose in religion, one that thinks he may doe what he listeth

libell, a writing, or booke

librarie, a studie, a great number of bookes

licentious, taking libertie to doe euill

ligate, bound, tyed

ligament, the string tying the bones together

linage [fr], stocke, kinred

limitation, appointment, how farre any thing shall goe, restraining:

limber, britle

limit, bounds, border, or land marke, also to set such bounds. &c.

liniament, a forme, or proportion by lines, that are drawne

lingell, shoemakers threed

linquist, skilfull in tongues

linquish, to leaue or forsake

lint, cloth

liquide, moist, melted:

literature, learning

litigious, quarrellous, full of strife

lieuetenant, [fr] deputie in anothers place

lithernesse, slouthfulnes, idlenes

loame, earth, or morter

logicall, [gr] belonging to reason

longitude, length

lore, lawe

lotarie, [fr] casting of lots.

lourdin, [fr] rude, clownish

loyall, [fr] obedient, trustie, constant

lumber, old stuffe

lunatick, wanting his wits, at a certaine time of the age of the moone

lumpish, sad or sower countenance.

lustre, glistering, shinning

luxurious, riotous, and excessiue in pleasure, and wontonnesse.

M

MAcerate, to steepe in water, or make cleane

madefie, dip, make wet

maffle, stammer, or stut

magicke, inchaunting, coniuring

magistrate, gouernour

magitian, [gr] one vsing witchcraft

magnanimitie, valientnes, courage

magnificence, sumptuousnes

magnifie, to extoll, or praise highly

magnitude, greatnes

mayre, [fr] leane

maiestie, the stately port and honourable renowne of any

maladie, [fr] disease

malecontent, [fr] discontented

malediction, slaundring, ill report, or backbiting, or cursing

malefactor, an euill doer

malepert, saucy, proud, snappish

maligne, [fr] to hate, with purpose to hurt

malignitie, [fr] naughtines, malice

malitious, hating, or enuying

manchet, fine white breade

mandate, a charge, or commaundement

maniacque, [fr] mad: braine sick

manicle, a fetter, for to bind the hands

manifest, opened, declared or reuealed

manuring, dung, tilling

mannage, [fr] handle

mansion, an abiding place

manuall, done with the hand

manumisse, to set free, or at libertie

maranatha, [gr] accursed

marche, [fr] goe in aray, or goe forward

margent, edge, or brim of any thing

marte, [fr] a faire

massacre, [fr] kill, put to death

martiall, warlike, or valiant, or taking paines and delight in
   warres

martyre, [gr] witnes, one suffering death for the faith of Christ

materiall, of some matter, or importance.

matrixe, wombe

matron, an auncient, sober, and a discreete woman.

mature, ripe, perfect, speedy

maugre, [fr] despight, against ones will

maxime, a principle, or sure ground in any matter

mechanicall,
mechanick,   } [gr] handie craft.

mediatour, aduocate, or surety, or one making peace betwixt two

medicine, remedie, or cure

mediocritie, a measure, a meane

meditate, muse vpon, bethinke

meditation, the earnest minding or thinking vpon a thing

melancholie, [gr] black choler, a humor of solitarines, or sadnes

mellifluous, sweete as hony, yielding much hony.

melody, [gr] sweete sounding, or sweete musick

memorable, worthie to be remembred

menace, [fr] to threaten

menstruous, defiled, or foule.

mentall, belonging to the minde

mercenary, seruing for wages, and hireling.

meridian, pertaining to noone tide

meritorious, that deserueth, or set for advauntage.

metamorphosis, [gr] a changing of one shape, or likenes into
  another

metaphor, [gr] similitude, or the putting ouer of a word from
  his proper and naturall signification, to a forraine or vnproper
  signification.

meteors, [gr] elementarie bodies, or moyst things, ingendered of
  vapours in the ayre aboue.

method, [gr] an order, or readie way to teach, or doo any thing

methodized, [gr] brought into order

metropolitane, [gr] of the chiefe citty.

microcosme, [gr] a little world

militant, warring, or beeing in warres.

miguionise, [fr] play the wanton:

ministration, ministring, or seruice, or charge to doo a thing:

minoritie, a mans time vnder age

minutly, smally:

miraculous, meruailous, or wonderfull:

mirrour, [fr] a looking-glasse

miscreants, infidels, mis-beleeuers:

misprission, concealement of a mans owne knowledge.

misknow, to mistake purposely, to be ignorant of.

mitigate, asswage, qualifie, or pacifie

mixtion,
mixture, } mingling, or tempering together.

mobilitie, moouing or stirring.

modell, measure,

moderate, temperate, or keeping a meane,

moderation, keeping due order and proportion:

moderne, [fr] of our time

modest, sober, demure

moitie, [fr] halfe.

molestation, troubling

mollifie, make soft

momentanie, that which lasteth but a while:

moment, weight, or importance, also a short time

monarch, [gr] one ruling all the kingdoms about him

monarchie, [gr] the rule of one prince alone:

monasterie, [gr] colledge of monks

monopolie, [gr] a licence that none shall buy and sell a thing, but one alone.

monument, a remembrance of some notable act, as Tombs

moosell, to fetter

moote, [fr] argue, or dispute a case in law

moralitie, ciuill behauiour.

morall, pertaining to manners, behauior, and life, among men

morgage, [fr] lay to pawne

morigerous, well mannered

mortall, that endeth ere hauing an end, and dying deadly:

mortifie, kill, or make dead, and sencelesse.

mortuarie, dutie paid for the dead,

motiue, cause moouing, or the thing, and reason, that mooueth to doe any thing.

mouldre, [fr] make small, turne to dust

mulct, a fine, penaltie, or punishment:

multiplicitie, varietie, or diuersitie of sorts.

mundifie, to make cleane:

munition, defence, supportation, or strength, and plentie of weapons, to resist in warre.

municipall, priuately belonging to a freeman, or burgesse of a cittie.

muses, [gr] goddesses of learning.

mustaches, [fr] the hayre of the vpper lippe.

mutable, changeable, wauering.

mutation, change.

muthologie, [gr] expounding of the tales of the Poets.

mutilate, wanting some part, maimed

mutuall, one for another

myrrhe, [gr] sweet gumme

mysterie, [gr] a secret, or hid thing:

mysticall, [gr] that hath a misterie in it.

N

NArration, declaration, or report.

nationall, belonging, or consisting of a nation, or kingdome.

natiue, where one was borne, or naturall.

natiuitie, birth, or the day of birth

nauigable, where ships may safely passe, or that may be sailed vpon.

nauigation, sayling, or passing by water

necromancie, [gr] blacke art, or coniuring, by calling vpon spirits.

nectar, a pleasant drinke, which is feyned to be the drinke of the gods.

negatiue, that denieth

negotiation, trafficke, or busines

neotericke, [gr] one of late time

nevewe, [fr] a sonne or daughters sonne

nerue, sinewe

nete, [fr] fine

neutrall,
neuter, } of neither side:

nice, [fr] slow, laysie

nicholaitan, [gr] an heretike, like Nicholas, who helde that wiues should bee common to all alike.

nominate, to name, or appoint

nonage, [fr] a childs time, vnder age

nonresidence, vnnecessary and wilfull absence, of any one from his place or charge:

nonsuite, [fr] not following, or the ending and giuing ouer of a suite

notable, worthy, meete to be regarded and esteemed:

notarie, Scriuener, or register

notifie, to make knowne, or to giue warning of.

notion, inwarde knowledge, or vnderstanding:

notorious, knowne to all, or made plaine and manifest.

noyance, hurt.

noysome, hurtfull,

nullitie, nothing

numeration, numbring

nuncupatory, telling, or declaring any thing.

nuptiall, belonging to marriage

nutriment, nourishment

O

Obdurate, harden, or to make more hard

obeisance, [fr] obedience

obiect, laide, or set against, or that whereon any thing resteth, or that where any thing is occupied, or set a worke.

oblation, offering

oblectation, recreation, delight

obliged, bound, or beholden

oblique, crooked, ouerthwart

obliuious, forfetfull

obloquie, euill report

obnoxious, faultie, subiect to danger

obnubilate, to make darke.

obscæne, bawdie, filthy, ribauldrie

obscure, darke, or cloudie

obsequious, seruiceable, readie at hand

obseruant, dutifull, full of diligent seruice.

obsession, besieging, or compassing about

obsolete, olde, past date, growne out of vse or custome.

obstacle, hinderance or let

obstinate, froward, stubberne, or stiffe in his owne opinion

obstruction, stopping, repressing

obtestate, humble, to beseech, or to call to witnesse:

obtrectation, slaunder, euill report.

obtuse, dull or blunt:

occidentall, belonging to the west

occluding, shutting fast:

occurrences, [fr] occasions, things that offer themselues by the
    way:

ocean, [gr] the maine sea

odious, hateful, disdainfull

odor, smell, sent, or sauour:

odoriferous, sweet smelling

oeconomicke, [gr] things that pertaine to houshold affaires

offensiue, giuing offence, offering wrong, or displeasing

officiall, belonging to an office,

officious, dutifull, dilligent, very readie or willing to please.

oligarchie, [gr] a Common-wealth, where two Princes equall
    haue all the authoritie.

oliuet, place of Oliues:

ombrage, [fr] shade, harbor, or bower to rest vnder.

ominous, that signifieth some good, or ill lucke:

omit, let passe, ouerslip.

omnipotent, almightie, great, or high

omni-scient, knowing all things

onerous, burdenous, or chargeable

onust, loaden, ouercharged

operation,
operatiue, } working, or effect

opinionate, hauing a good opinion of, or standing on his owne
opinion

oportunitie, fitnes to any thing,

oppilation, stopping

oppose, set againe

opposite, contrarie, or set ouer against

oppressed, grieued, or violently wronged:

opprobrious, reprochfull, to taunt, reuile, or vpbraide with bad
speeches.

oppugne, to labour against, to resist

option, choosing or wishing

oracle, [gr] a speech or aunswere giuen from God:

oratorie, eloquent speech:

ordination, ordeyning

ordure, dung, filth,

orifice, mouth

originall, the first, or such as it was at the beginning

organe, [gr] an instrument to doo any thing with:

ornament, a decking, adorning, or trimming.

orphant, [gr] a childe without parents

ossicle, bone:

ostages, [fr] pledges giuen and taken

ostentation, boasting

orthographie, [gr] true writing

ouerplus, [fr] more then needeth

outragious, [fr] fierce, vnreasonable.

P

PAcifie, to make quiet.

pactation, a couenanting or bargayning.

palatine, [fr] belonging to a Princes Court, or pallace.

palinodie, [gr] a recanting, or vnsaying of any thing

palpable, that may be felt, manifest:

pamphlet, a small treatise, or booke

parable, [gr] similitude, or an applying of some thing to our matter, fitly alleaged, for some likenesse which it hath to our purpose.

paradise, [gr] place of pleasure

paradoxe, [gr] marueilous, or strange speech:

paragon, [fr] patterne, example

paraleles, [gr] lines, or other things as farre off from one another, in one place as in another.

paramour, an amorous louer

paraphrase, [gr] exposition of any thing by many words.

parasite, [gr] a base flatterer, or soothing companion:

parenthesis, [gr] a clause contayned in another sentence:

paricide, a murtherer of parents

parle, [fr] speech, or conference.

parsimonie, thriftines, sparing

participate, partake, deuide, or distribute, to giue, or take part:
particularize, to deuide into parts, and to handle euery particuler.
partition, deuision.
passeouer, one of the Jewes feasts, in remembrance of Gods
    passing ouer them, when he slewe so many of the Egiptians
passion, suffering, griefe
pastorall, belonging to sheapheards
patheticall, [gr] vehement, full of passions, or mouing affections
patriarke, [gr] chiefe father
patrimonie, fathers, gift, or goods left by a father
patronage, [fr] defence, protection
patronise, defend
paucitie, fewnes, or smale number
pause, thinke, stay, or rest
pauillion, [fr] tente
peerelesse, worthie, vnmatchable
peccaui, I haue offended.
peccant, offending, doing amisse
peculiar, proper, or specially belonging
pecuniarie, coyne
pellicles, skinnes
penetrable, that may be pearsed
penitentiarie, one repenting, or doing pennaunce.
penaltie, losse
pension, [fr] payment, yearely fee
pensiue, [fr] sorrowfull
pentecost, [gr] whitsontide

penurie, want or extreame neede
perambulation, a walking about
peregrination, iourneing in a strange land
peremptorie, resolute, short
perforations, holes, or pierced through
perfidious, trayterous, vnfaithfull
perfricated, rubbed much
perilous, dangerous
periclitation, ieopardie, or hazarding
period, [gr] the end of a perfect sentence
periurie, forswearing, or breaking of ones oath.
permanent, continuing, or a biding till the end
permission, sufferance, leaue
permit, suffer, giue leaue
permutable, changable
pernitious, dangerous, hurtfull
perpendicular, directly, downe right
perpetrate, to commit, or doe
perpetuitie, continuance for euer
perplexitie, troublesome, griefe, distresse, doubtfulnes
persecute, trouble, afflict, or pursue after.
persist,
perseuer, } continew, constantly, and resolutely.
personate, to counterfaite, anothers person
perspicacie, quicknes of sight, vnderstanding
perspicuous, euedent, cleare, that may bee seene through
pertinacie, obstinacie, stifnes in opinion

perturbation, disquietnes, or trouble

peruerse, froward, mischeiuous

peruert, ouerthrowe, or turne vp side downe

pese, [fr] to weigh

peruicacie, obstinacie, stifneckednes

pesant, [fr] clowne

pester, filled

pest, the plague, or pestilence

pestiferous, contagious, hurtfull

petition, prayer, or request

pettigree, [fr] stock, or ofspring

petulancie, wantonnes, saucines.

phantasie, [gr] imagination

philacteries, [gr] scroles of parchment, whereon, was writen the
    tenne commaundements.

physiognomie, [gr] knowledge of a mans nature by his visage,
    and countenance

physicke, [gr] medicine, helping, or curing

phlebotomie, [gr] letting bloud

phrase, [gr] forme of speach

philosophie, [gr] study of wisdome

phrensie, [gr] madnes

pietie, godliness, holines

pillage, [fr] spoile in warre, and sacking, of the enemies.

pinguiditie, fatnes, or greasinesse

pilot, [fr] maister, guider of a ship

pionner, [fr] digger, or ditcher

piramis, [gr] ⎫ a steeple, or other building, or a pillar broade
piramides,　⎭ beneath, and sharpe aboue

pistated, baked

pirate, [fr] a robber on the sea

pittance, [fr] short, banquet

placable, easie to be pleased

planet, [gr] wandring starre

plaintife, [fr] the partie complayning

plausible, pleasing, or receiued ioyfully, and willingly

plenitude, fulnes, thicknesse

plonge, [fr] dippe, or put vnder the water

plume, feather

pluralitie, more then one

pluuiatile, raine

poeme, [gr] verses of a poet

poet, [gr] a verse maker

poetesse, a woman poet

pole, [gr] the end of the axeltree whereon the astronomers, faine
　the heauens to be turned.

pollicie, a wittie shift

poligamie, [gr] hauing moe wiues then one

polish, to deck, or make faire, smooth, sleeke, or shining

pollute, defile, or distaine, or make filthie

pomegarnet, or **pomegranet**, [k] fruite

pompe, the countenance of things in furniture, and setting foorth
　to the outward shewe.

ponderous, weightie, heauie

pontificall, lordly, sumptuous, bishop-like.

portable, that may be carried with ease.

popular, seeking the fauour of the people by all meanes possible:

populus, full of people:

popularitie, pleasing the people,

position, a question to be disputed of

posteritie, they that come after by birth: the age after vs.

postscript, written after

potion, a drinke,

pourtrait, [fr] draw the forme, or proportion of a thing

practicall, [gr]

practique, } practising.

pragmaticall,

preamble, [fr] forespeech, a flourish, entrance, or assay.

precedent, going before

precept, a rule giuen, an admonition, or commaundement.

precinct, compasse appointed:

predecessor, one that was in place before another.

predestinate, to appoint before.

prediction, afore telling, or prophecying

predominante, ruling

preheminence, excellent, rule, authoritie ouer others

preface, a speech before the matter it selfe

prefigurate, forshewe by a figure

prefixed, set in the fore part

pregnant, wittie, substantiall, with child,

preiudicate, giuing his iudgment, before he knoweth the man, or
    matter

preiudice, hindering ones cause, sentence, an opinion deliuered
before knowledge of any thing

preludium, an entrance to any thing

premeditation, thinking of a matter before hand

premunire, [fr] forfeiture of goods

preoccupation, a preuenting by speech or other wayes

preordination, appointing before

preparatiue, that which maketh fit or prepareth

preposterous, disorder, froward, topsiteruie, setting the cart
before the horse, as we vse to say

prerogatiue, priuiledge, or authoritie before another

presage, to tell before, to betoken, to foresee.

presbitarie, [gr] eldership

prescience, foreknowledge

prescript, decree, or assignement

prescription, limitation, or appointing a certaine compasse.

preseruatiue, that which defendeth

president, a chiefe, ruler next vnder the highest

prest, reacte

presuppose, faine a thing to be before it is.

pretermit, to passe ouer, to forget willinglie.

preterlapsed, passed, or gone past

pretext, an excuse, colour, or pretence

preuarication, collusion, or betraying of a cause or matter, for
want of more earnest speech.

primitiue,
primarie, } first, or formost, or excellent.

prioritie, being in the formost place, or in greater excellencie and
    superioritie then another.

pristine, old, wonted, or accustomed

priuation, depriuing, vtter taking away, or withdrawing

priuiledge, prerogatiue, or liberty, more then others haue

probable, that may be easilie proued to be true.

probation, alouance, tryall

probleme, [gr] proposition, or sentence in manner of a question.

proceede, goe forth, or goe forward,

processe, proceeding, passing forward,

procliuitie, inclination to any thing

proctour, a factour, or solicitor.

procrastinate, to defer, or delay

prodigall, too riotous in spending

prodigious, wonderfull, giuing an ill signe.

prodition, betraying, treason

profane, vngodly, not consecrated, or vnhallowing that which was
    holy.

profound, deepe, or high.

profunditie, deepenes.

profusion, pouring out wastfully,

progenie, ofspring, generation, or issue of children.

progenitor, a fore-father, or grandfather.

prognosticate, [gr] to know or giue out before-hand, or to tell
    afore-hand what shall happen.

grogresse, a going forward:

prohibit, to forbid, or giue straight charge to the contrary.

proiect, a plot, or wise contriuing of any thing, or casting forth

prolixe, tedious, long, or large.

prolocutor, a speaker for another

prologue, a preface, or forespeech

prolong, stretch out, or defer.

promerit, desert:

promote, to honor or aduaunce to greater dignitie, and higher place

prompt, ready, quicke:

promulgation, publishing openly, or proclaiming.

prone, ready, or inclining

prowesse, [fr] valiantnesse

propagate, to enlarge, or multiply.

prophecie, [gr] foretell, or expound

prophet, [gr] he that prophecieth

propitiation, a sacrifice to appease Gods displeasure:

propitiatorie, that which reconcileth, or which purchaseth mercie, at the mercie seate:

propitious, not displeased, fauourable

proportion, equalnes, measure:

propose, propound, set before, or shew

proprietie, propertie, owing, or challenging as his owne, and none others:

proroge, put off, prolong, deferre

proscription, a condemnation, or banishment proclaimed, or an open sale.

prose, that writing which is not verse.

proselite, [gr] stranger conuerted to our religion or manners:

prosequute, follow after, or finish

prospect, a sight a farre off.

prostitute, set open for vncleanesse, to set foorth to sale.

prostrate, to cast downe, or fall downe flat on the ground.

protect, defend, saue, or couer:

protest, to affirme, and declare openly:

protract, deferre, or prolong, or draw out at length:

prouident, foreseeing with wise consideration, and prouiding aforehand

prouinciall, iurisdiction, belonging to a prouince, or outcountry

prouocation, prouoking, enforcing, vrging pressing, or alluring

prudence, wisdome, wittinesse

publicane, a farmer, or common man of a Cittie:

pulers, [fr] dust, or pouders

puluirisated, beaten, or broken into dust, or powder.

purifie, purge, scoure, or make cleane

pursuit, [fr] following after

putrifie, to waxe rotten, or corrupted as a sore.

pulsillanimitie, faint-hartednes, cowardlinesse.

puissant, [fr] strong, valiant

Q

QVadrangle, foure-cornered

quadrant,
quadrate, } foure square, or a quarter.

quartane, belonging to, or comming euery fourth day.

queach, thicke heape

querimonious, full of complaining, and lamentation:

quintessence, [fr] chiefe vertue, drawne by art out of many compounds together.

quondam, heeretofore, in times past

quote, [fr] cite, preuent

quotidian, daily, that happeneth euery day.

R

RAcha, fie, a note of extreame anger, signified by the gesture of the person that speaketh it, to him that he speaketh to.

radicall, partaining to the roote, naturall:

radiant, shining bright:

rallie, [fr] gather together men dispersed, and out of order.

rampar, [fr] fortification, or trench

rapacitie,
rapine, } violent, catching, extortion, or pillage, or rauening.

raritie, scarsenes, fewnes

ratifie, establish, or confirme

rauish, [fr] take away by force,

raunged, [fr] ordered, or put into order

reachlesse, carelesse, or negligent:

reall, substantiall, or that is indeed subsisting:

recantation, an vnsaying of that which was said before

recapitulation, a briefe rehearsing againe of any thing

receptacle, a place to receiue things in

reciprock, or
reciprocall, } that hath respect back a gaine to the same thing.

recite, rehearse, or repeate

reclaime, to gainesay, or call back againe:

recognissance, [fr] acknowledging, or a signe of acknowledging, and confessing any thing.

recoile, [fr] goe backe.

reconcile, bring into fauour, or to make peace betwixt.

records, writings layde vp for remembrance:

recreate, refresh, comfort,

recourse, a running backe againe

rectifie, to make right or straight

redeeme, purchase, buy againe, or raunsome.

redemption, a buying againe

redresse, [fr] correct, amend.

reduce, to bring back againe

reduction, a bringing backe

redundant, ouerflowing, or abounding too much.

reduplicated, doubled.

reedifie, build vp againe

reestablish, to settle againe as before

refection, a refreshing, or recreating.

refell, to confute, or proue false

reference, a pointing at, or alluding to

referre, put ouer, or to report himselfe vnto.

refine, repaire, renue, or amend

reflection, casting backe, or bowing, turning backe againe

refractarie, wilful in opinion, obstinate.

refraine, [fr] abstaine from, keepe in

refuge, succour, or place of safetie

refulgent, shining bright

refute, to disproue

regall, princly, like a King

regenerate, borne againe

regeneration, a new birth,

regent, a Gouernor, or Ruler

regiment, gouernment, guidance, rule, or dominion.

register, kalender, a reckoning booke

regrator, huckster, or one that buyeth any thing, and trims it vp
   to make it more salable.

regresse, returning backe againe

reguler, made according to rule and order.

reiect, fling, cast away, or refuse

reioynder [fr], a thing added afterwards, or is when the defendant
   maketh answere to the replication of the plaintife.

reiterate, to doo, or repeate againe the same thing often.

relapse, back-sliding.

relate, report, rehearse, or declare

relation, pointing, reporting, or referring

relatiue, hauing relation vnto

relaxation, refreshing, releasing,

release, free, quit:

reliefe, [fr] ayde, helpe, or succour.

reliques, the remainder.

relinquish, to leaue, or forsake

relish, tast:

remarkable, able or worthy to be marked againe:

remisse, loose, negligent, or dull, or too fauourable.

remit, forgiue, release, or acquite.

remorse, [fr] prick of conscience

remote, set a farre of

remuneration, rewarding, or requiting

renouate, renew, or repaire

renounce, forsake, or resigne

renoume, [fr] credite, fame, report

reparation, a renewing

repast, [fr] foode

repeale, [fr] call backe againe

repell, to put, or thrust backe

repercussiue, striking, or rebounding back againe.

replenish, fill:

replete, filled full

repleueying, redeeming of a gage, or any thing in prison:

replie, to confirme a speech before vttered.

repose, [fr] put, wholly to rest

represent, expresse, beare shew of a thing

represse, put downe, to let or stop

reprobate, a cast away, out of fauour, a forlorne person, and one
    past grace

reproch, [fr] shame, disgrace

republicke, a Common-wealth

repugnancie, contrarietie, or disagreement

repugnant, contrarie

repugne, to resist, oppose, stand against

repulse, to put, or driue backe

repute, account, or esteeme:

requisite, required as necessary:

reserue, to keepe for the time to come

resident, abiding or continuing in his place.

resignation, a yeelding vp, or restoring of anie thing.

resigne, giue ouer to another

resist, withstand

resolue, to vnloose, to satisfie, to purpose constantly,

resort, [fr] accesse, or comming to

respiration, breathing out.

respite, [fr] defer, or delay the time, to breath in:

resplendent, shining bright

responses, answers.

restauration, restoring, or reuiuing

restitution, restoring, satisfaction

restrained, beeing held in, or brideled

resume, take againe

retire, [fr] to giue backe, or goe back

reteyne, keepe backe

retort, to turne, or wrest backward

retract, [fr] going backe

retrograde, going backward

reuell, [fr] play the wanton

reuerend, worthy of reuerence

reueale, lay open, disclose, or make known a matter of secret

reuert, to returne

reuenewe, [fr] rents comming in

reuoke, to call backe, or draw back

reuolt, [fr] forsake one, to goe to another his enemie:

reuolue, to tosse vp and downe, to determine well of in the mind

rhetorician, [gr] learned and skilfull in rhetoricke.

rhetoricke, [gr] art of eloquence

rheume, [gr] or **catarre**, a distilling of humours from the head

ridiculous, that deserueth to be laughed at in scorne.

rifle, [fr] search, take away by violence

rigorous, cruell, and hard

rinse, [fr] wash, make cleane by washing

riuall, [fr] one suing, and striuing for the same thing.

rubrick, a lawe, or title

royalty, [fr] gouernment, rule, authority

rudiment, first instruction, or principle

rubicunde, red, or ruddie

ruinous, ready to fall

ruminate, to chewe ouer againe, to studie earnestlie vppon

runnagate, one that runneth away, and wandreth abroad.

rupture, breach, or bursting

rurall,
rusticall, } clownish, vplandish, or churlish, and vnmannerly

S

saboth, rest

sacrament, holie signe, oath, or misterie

sacred, holy, consecrated

sacrifice, an offering

sacrificule, a little offering

sacriledge, church robbing, the stealing of holy things

safeconduit, [fr] safe keeping or safe guiding

sagacitie, sharpnes of wit, witnes

saint, holy one

sallie, [fr] to step out from the rest of the armie, to make a skermish

saluation, a sauing

salubritie, wholesomnes

sanctifie, hallowe, make holy, or keepe holy

sanctification, holines

sanctitie,
sanctmonie, } holines.

sanctuarie, holy place, saue, defend

sandals, [gr] slippers

sanguine, bloudy, or of the colour of bloud.

sanitie, health, or soundnes

sapience, wisdome

satiate, filled, satisfied

satietie, fulnes, plentie

satisfaction, a making amends for wrongs, or displeasures

satisfactorie, that dischargeth, or answereth for

saturate, filled, or glutted

saturitie, fulnesse, or plentifulnesse

sauage, [fr] wild, cruell, or rude

satyre, [gr] a nipping and scoffing verse

satericke,
satiricall, } belonging to a scoffing verse.

scandalize, [gr] to offend, or giue occasion, to mislike

scandall, [gr] an offence, or stumbling block

scarifie, [fr] to launce, or open a sore

scedule, [fr] obligation, or bill of ones hand.

schisme, breach, or diuision in matters of religion

schismatike, that maketh a schisme

science, knowledge, or skill

scripture, writing

scruple, doubt, difficultie

scrutiny, dilligent search, inquiry

scrupulous, full of doubts

scurrilitie, saucie, scoffing

seclude, shutout, or put a part

sectarie, one whom many other doe followe in opinion.

sect, a diuersitie in opinion from others

section, a deuision, or parting

secular, worldly, of the world

secundarie, the second, or of the second sort

securitie, carelessenes, feare of nothing

sediment, that which sinketh to the bottome.

seditious, making contention

seduce, deceiue, or deuide, or leade aside

sedulitie, dilligence or carefulnes

segniorie, [fr] lordship

segregate, to set a part, or seperate

seize, [fr] to forfaite to the prince

select, to choose out from others

semicircle, halfe a circle, or compasse

seminarie, a nurserie, or seede plot for young trees, or grafts

senator, alderman, or counsailer

sense, feeling, or perceiuing

sensible, easily felt, or perceiued

sensuall, brutish, pertaining to the flesh, and bodily sence

sententious, full of fine sentences, and speeches.

sentinell, [fr] watching by night

seperation, deuiding, seuering, or parting one from another

sepulcher, graue, or tombe

sepulte, burie, or lay in the ground

sequele, following, or that which followeth.

sequester, to put into an indifferent mans hands, to deuide, keepe
    or iudge of

serious, earnest, or of waight, and importance

serpentine, of, or like a serpent

seruile, slauish

seruitude, bondage, or slauery

seuere, sharpe, curst, or cruell

seueritie, sharpnes, roughnes

sex, kind

shackle, fetter

significant, plainely signifying

similie, or,
similitude, } likenes, or resemblance.

simonie, [fr] when spirituall matters, are bought, and solde for money

simplicitie, plainenes

sinister, vnhappie, bad, vnlawefull, or contrarie.

sincere, pure, vncorrupt, vnmingled, or without dissimulation

singularitie, being like no body else, in opinion, or other wayes

situation, setting, or standing of any place.

sleight, guile, craft, or subtiltie.

smatterer, some what learned, or one hauing but a little skill

snatch, to take hastely

snipperings, pairings

soare, [fr] mount high

sociall, or } fellowe like, one that wil keepe company, or one
sociable, } with whom a man may easily keepe company.

societie, fellowship, company

sodomitrie, when one man lyeth filthylie with another man

soiourne, [fr] remaine in a place

solace, comfort

solemnize, to doe a thing with great pompe, reuerence, or
   deuotion

solicite, [fr] moue

solide, sound, heauie, not hollowe

solitarie, alone, or without company

solution, vnloosing, or paying

sophister, [gr] cauiller, or craftie disputer

sophistikation,
sophisme, } a cauilling, deceitfull speech.

sotte, [fr] foole, dunse

soueraigne, [fr] chiefe, or highest in authoritie.

source, [fr] waue, or issuing foorth of water

soile, [fr] foule, or durtie

spatious, large, wide, or broade

specifie, signifie, or declare particularly

specke, spot, or marke

spectacle, a thing to be looked at

sperme, seede

sphære, [gr] round circle, or any thing that is round

spicerie, a place to keepe spice in

splendent, glistering, shinning

splene, milt

spongeous, like a sponge

spousals, betrothings, or contracts

spume, fome, or froth

stabilitie, surenes, certaine, strong

stable, sure, stedfast

stablished, sure, confirmed, one made strong

station, a standing place

statue, an image of wood, or any other matter

stature, height, bignes

sterilitie, barrennes

stigmaticall, [gr] knauish, noted for a lewd naughty fellowe, burnt through the eare for a rogue.

stile, manner, or forme of speech, or writing

stillatorie, a distilling place

stipendarie, one that serueth for wages

stipulation, a solemne couenant

strangle, kill, or hang

stratageme, a pollicie, or wittie shift in warre

strict, straight, seuere, or sharpe.

strictnes, narrownes, or smalenes

studius, dilligent, desirous of learning.

stupefie, to astonish

stupiditie, astonishment, dulnes

suasorie, containing counsaile and exhortation

subalterne, succeeding, following by course and order.

subdued, kept vnder, or brought in subiection

sublimity, height, highnes

sublime, set on high, lift vp

submisse, lowly, humble, brought in subiection

suborne, [fr] to procure false witnes

subscribe, write vnder, or to agree with another in any matter

subsequent, following hard by

subsiste, to abide, or haue a being

substitute, a deputie, or one set in place of another.

substract,
subtract, } take from, withdrawe.

subtill, craftie, wilie, deceitfall

subuerte, to turne vpside downe, to destroy.

succeede, followe, or come in anothers place

successor, he that comes in place of another

succincte, shorten, or briefe, or close girt vp

suggest, prompt, tell priuily, or put in mind of.

suffixed, fastened vnto

suffocate, to choake vp, or strangle

suffragane, a bishops deputie, or helper

suffrage, consent, or voice, or helpe

suggest, a high place, or pulpit

sulphure, brimstone

summarie, [fr] an abridgement, or thing drawne into a lesse compasse

summarilie, briefely, in fewe words

sumptuous, [fr] costly, rich

supererogation, giuing more then is required.

superabundant,
superfluous, } needelesse, vnnecessarie ouer much, that which runneth ouer.

superficies, vpper side, or out side

superficiall, taking onely the outside, and vttermost part

superioritie, place aboue another

superscription, writing aboue

superstitious, fearefull in matters of religion without cause, one giuen to false and vaine religion

supplant, ouerthrowe, or trippe, with the feete.

supplement, that which maketh vp, or addeth that which wanteth in any thing

supple, [fr] make soft, or gentle

supplication, request, or prayer

suppliant, [fr] humbly intreating

support, beare vp, or conuaie vnder

supposition, supposing, thinking, iudging, or imagining.

suppresse, keepe downe, conceale, or keepe secret

supreme, the highest, or greatest

supremacie, chiefedome, or highest place in authoritie aboue all others

surcease, [fr] to giue ouer, or cease

surcharge, [fr] ouercharge, hurt

surmount, [fr]
surpasse, } exceede, or goe beyond.

surplus, more then inough

surprise, [fr] to come vpon, and vnawares, and to take of a suddaine.

surrender, to yield vp to another

surrogate, [fr] a deputie in anothers place

suruiue, [fr] ouer liue, or liue after

suspense, doubt, or vncertaintie

sustained, suffered, or endured

swaine, clowne

swarth, darke, or blackish

swarue, goe awry erre.

sycophant, [gr] tale bearer or false accuser.

symball, [gr] creede

symmetrie, [gr] a due proportion of one part with another

sympathie, [gr] fellowelike feeling.

symptome, [gr] any griefe, or passion, following a disease

synagogue, [gr] place of assemblie

synode, [gr] a generall assemblie, or meeting

T

Tablet, [fr] little table

tabernacle, a tent, or pauilion

tacite, still, silent, saying nothing

taciturnite, silence, or keeping counsaile

tapish, [fr] lie downe, hide it selfe

taxed, seised, appointed to pay a subsidie

temerarious, rash, vnaduised, or haire braine

temeritie, rashnes, vnaduisednes

temperance, sobrietie, moderation

temperate, keeping a meane, moderate

temperature,
temperament, } temperatenes, meane, or due proportion.

tempestuous, boisterous, or stormie

temporall, that which indureth but for a certaine time

temporarie, for a time

temporise, to serue the time, or to followe the fashions, and behauiour of the time.

tenacitie, nigardnes

tenuitie, smalenesse, or slendernesse

tenure, [fr] hold, or manner of holding a possession

termination, ending, finishing, or bounding

teritorie, [fr] region, or the countrie lying about the citie.

tertian, belonging to euery third day

terrestriall, earthly

testament, last will

testification, witnessing

testimonies, records, depositions or witnessings.

tetrarch, [gr] gouernour, or prince of a fourth part, of a country

theologie, [gr] diuinitie, the science of liuing blessedly for euer

theoricke, [gr] the contemplation, or inward knowledge, of any art

throne, [gr] a kings seate, or chaire of estate.

throtle, strangle, hang, or torment

thwart, crosse, or mock

thwite, shaue

timerous, fearefull, abashed

timiditie, fearefulnes

tincture, a colour, die, or staining

tolerable, that which may be suffered

tone, [gr] a tune, note, or accent

trace, [fr] find out by the foote steppes

tractable, easie to handle, or easie to be entreated

tractate, a treatise, or booke, handling any matter

tracte, [fr] a space, or length

tradition, a deliuering from one to another.

traduce, to slaunder, reproach, or defame, to bring in, or drawe from one to another.

traffique, [fr] bargayning

tragedian, a maker, or player, of a tragedy.

tragedie, [gr] a solemne play, describing cruell murders and sorrowes

tragicall, cruell, sorrowfull, like a tragedy.

traine, [fr] followers, company

tranquilitie, quietnes, or calmenes, or rest

transcendent, climing ouer, mounting vp

transferre, conceiue ouer

transforme,
transfigure, } change from one fashion, to another

transgresse, breake, offende or goe ouer

transitorie, [fr] soone passing away, not long lasting.

translation, altering, chaunging

transmigration, a passing from one place, to dwell in another.

transmutation, a change from one place, to another

transome, lintell ouer a dore

transparent, that which may bee seene through

transport, carie ouer, from one place to another.

transpose, change

transubstantiation, a changing of one substance into another

trauerse, [fr] strike, or thrust through

triangle,
triangular, } three cornered.

tribe, a company, ward, or hundred

tribulation, [fr] trouble, sorrowe, anguish

tribunall, iudgement seate

tributarie, [fr] that payeth tribute

tribute, [fr] rent, pension, or subsidie

tripartite, threefold, or deuided into three parts.

triuiall, common, of smale estimation

triumph, great ioy outwardly shewed

triumphant, reioycing for the conquest

trompe, [fr] deceiue

troncheon, stake, or billet

trophee, a victorie, or any thing set in signe of victorie

tropickes, [gr] circles in the heauen which when the sunne comes too, beginnes to returne againe.

troupe, [fr] company, or band of men in an army

truce, peace

trucheman, an interpreter

truculent, cruell, or terrible in countenance.

trunchion, weapon.

tumult, vprore, hurly, burly or insurrection

tumultuous,
turbulent, } troublous, disturbing, or disquieting.

tiranize, vse crueltie

type, [gr] figure, example, shadowe of any thing.

V

Vacant, voyde, or emptie

vacation, a time of ceasing from labour

vagabonde, [fr] runnagate, one that will stay no where

validitie, strength, or force, or value

valour, force, courage, or strength

value, price, or estimation

vanquish, [fr] ouercome, preuaile, conquer, or ouerthrowe

vapor, moisture, ayre, hote breath, or reaking

varietie, change, or diuersitie

vassall, [fr] slaue, client

vaste, spoiled, destroyed, emptie

vauntcourers, [fr] forerunners

vbiquitie, presence of a person in all places.

varnish, shine

vegetable, springing, or growing, as herbes.

vehement, earnest, strong, forcible

vendible, saileable, easie, and readie to be solde

venerable, worshipfull, or reuerende

veneriall,
venerous, } fleshly, or lecherous, giuen to lecherie.

veniall, that which may be pardoned

vente, saleable

ventricle, the stomacke which receiues the meate

venuste, faire, beautifull

verbatim, word by word, perfectly

verbositie, much talking, and pratling

veritie, truth

verifie, to proue it to be true

versifie, make verses

vertigiousnes, lightnes, or a swimming of the heade

vestall, a nunne, vowing chastitie

vesture,
vestiment, } garment, attire, or clothing.

viand, [fr] victailes

viceroy, [fr] one set as a deputie in the Kings place.

vi[c]initie, neighbourhoode

vicegerent, one that supplyeth the place of another.

vicious, faultie, or full of vice

victorious, that hath gotten many victories.

viewe, behold, marke, or consider, or looke vppon

vigilance, watchfull, dilligence.

vigour, strength, courage, or force

vincible, that may be wonne, or easily ouercome.

vineyard, orchard of grapes

violate, to transgresse, defile, deflowre, or breake.

violent, forcible, cruell, iniurious:

viperine, like a viper, or of a viper.

virago, a woman of manly courage

virulent, full of poyson, venemous.

visage, [fr] face, forme, or shape.

vision, sight, apparition, or a phantasie.

visible, that may be seene

visitation, going to see

vitall, liuely, or pertayning to life.

vitiate, to corrupt, or deflower, and defile.

viuificent, liuely, or full of strength

viuifie, to quicken, or make aliue:

vlcer, bile, or botch

vlcerate, to blister, or make full of sores

vmpire, iudge:

vnconceaueable, not able to be conceiued

vnacessible, that cannot be come to.

vnanimitie, one consent of hart and mind

vnction, annointing

vndecent, vncomlie

vndermine, graue, dig

vnguent, an oyntment, or fat iuyce

vnitie,
vnion, } peace, or concord

vnitie, to make one thing of two, or moe, to couple, or ioyne:

vnsatiable, not content

vniformitie, one and the same fashion

vniuersall, generall, common:

vocall, with the voice, or pertaining to the voyce:

vocation, calling, estate, or trade of life.

vnsatiable, that neuer hath enough, neither can be satisfied:

volubilitie, swiftnes, or inconstancie

voluntary, of the owne accord, without being taught, or vrged.

voluptuous, giuen to pleasure

vpbraid, [fr] rise in ones stomach, cast in ones tæth:

vrbanitie, curtesie, good manners, or gentlenes:

vrgent, earnestly calling vpon, forcing

vsurpe, [fr] take vnlawfull authoritie, or to vse against right and reason.

vtensiles, [fr] things necessary for our vse in house-keeping, or in a trade.

vtilitie, profit

vlgar, common, much vsed

Z

ZOdiack, [gr] a circle in the heauen, wherein be placed the 12. signes, and in which the Sunne is mooued.

F I N I S .